The Carpenters

BY JOHN TOBLER

Copyright © 1998 O
(A Division of Book

Edited by Chris C
Cover & Book designed by Hilite D
Picture research b

ISBN: 0.711
Order No: (

Exclusive Distributors:
Book Sales Limited, 8/9 Frith Street, London W1V 5TZ, UK.
Music Sales Corporation, 257 Park Avenue South, New York, NY 10010, USA.
Music Sales Pty Limited, 120 Rothschild Avenue, Rosebery, NSW 2018, Australia.

To the Music Trade only:
Music Sales Limited, 8/9, Frith Street, London W1V 5TZ, UK.

Photo credits: Front cover: LFI. Other pictures supplied by Harry Goodwin and LFI.

Every effort has been made to trace the copyright holders of the photographs in this book but one or two were
unreachable. We would be grateful if the photographers concerned would contact us.

Printed in the United Kingdom by: Ebenezer Baylis & Son, Worcester.

A catalogue record for this book is available from the British Library.

Visit Omnibus Press at http://www.musicsales.co.uk

OMNIBUS PRESS
LONDON · NEW YORK · SYDNEY

Contents

Introduction

There have been many great non-classical female vocalists in the Twentieth Century, including (alphabetically) Gloria Estefan, Emmylou Harris, Olivia Newton-John, Dolly Parton, Linda Ronstadt, Diana Ross, Dusty Springfield, Barbra Streisand and Dionne Warwick, but none of these fabulous singers can equal the vocal quality of Karen Carpenter.

A word from Herb Alpert: "Karen was just an extremely nice person, she was a genuine person. I cared for her a great deal, we were friends, and that's how she was as an artist; she couldn't sing a song that she didn't like, and she knew what she was after: she was not a rock'n'roll singer, she wasn't a blues singer, she wasn't a jazz singer, she was what she presented. That's how she was as a person, very engaging, very upbeat, very sensitive, very nice to people that were responsible for furthering their career - never forgot a birthday, or a thank you to people all around this [record] company here - and she was loved. She was an extraordinary human being and I loved her. She had a magical sound and that's what I heard the first time I heard their rough tapes, her voice felt like it was in my lap - it was sitting in my lap, and it was very friendly and it was right next to me and it was somebody that I had known for a long time. And I think she communicated that to an enormous amount of people out there. We were touched by her, we were touched by this lady's soul."

Such is the morbid curiosity surrounding the fate of Karen Carpenter that the music she made with her brother Richard, impeccably arranged and produced songs that frequently topped the *Billboard* charts throughout the Seventies, is often overlooked. That they have been a household name for more than a quarter of a century is no mean achievement, but much of this can unfortunately be attributed to Karen Carpenter's death from anorexia nervosa in 1983, just four weeks before her 33rd birthday. Their music was enormously popular but The Carpenters were much more than pop stars: they were exceptionally talented musicians. Karen was a good drummer and a brilliant singer, whose perfect pitch meant that her guide vocals could often be used as finished recordings; Richard wrote, played, arranged and produced much of their material. Time for statistics: between 1970 and 1981, The Carpenters released ten original albums, seven of which were certified gold, and four of which reached the Top Five of the *Billboard* LP chart. In addition, *The Singles 1969 - 1973*, a compilation with a self-explanatory title, topped the *Billboard* chart, and was certified quadruple platinum. During the same period, the brother and sister team notched up 20 US hit singles, ten of which sold over a million copies, and a dozen of which reached the US Top Ten.

Richard Carpenter was born in New Haven, Connecticut, on October 15, 1946, and his sister, Karen, on March 2, 1950, also in New Haven. It was clear that Richard was a child prodigy, and his mastery, not only of the piano, but also of composition, producton and arrangement (both instrumentally and vocally), made it obvious that his career would be in music,

although not necessarily pop music.

Younger sister Karen was by all accounts a tomboy who idolised her brother. She was similarly bright, but was destined to be overshadowed; Richard was older, and therefore became successful before Karen, whose achievements were treated by her mother (by all accounts the dominant parent) simply as milestones which her brother had already reached. Research into anorexia has suggested that a common cause is low self-esteem on the part of the victim, and it has been further suggested that many victims of the disease are siblings to a parental favourite. However it would be wrong to presume that the fate of Karen Carpenter was simply the result of a lack of parental appreciation: while it is reasonable to assume that this was a contributory factor, there must have been many others which were equally significant.

By 1967, they were living in Downey, California, a middle-class suburb of Greater Los Angeles, and working in a jazz trio (completed by Wes Jacobs on bass and tuba). The trio were, by all accounts, hot stuff, hot enough in 1966 to win first prize at "The Battle Of The Bands", a significant amateur talent contest held at the Hollywood Bowl, but they really didn't look the part to sign with a major label at that time, and they failed an audition for RCA Records. A trio comprising a brother and sister/piano and drums duo, with a tuba player, performing mainly instrumentals might sound averagely psychedelic in the Nineties, but they were well out of step with the acid rock which was popular at the time. The Carpenters were determinedly a pop act who never aspired to rock stardom, and a generation of rock critics derided "The Downey Duo" (as they were unkindly dubbed in rock music Bible *Rolling Stone,*) for their wholesome, clean-living image, which was grossly unfashionable in an era when acts like The Rolling Stones, Led Zeppelin and The Who were the yardstick by which hipness was measured.

Even before the RCA fiasco, Karen had released a flop single, recorded and produced by Joe Osborn, a noted session musician who has appeared on literally hundreds of important pop and rock albums (including, the first five Carpenters LPs). When Richard Carpenter visited Osborn's studio to help a friend from university at a recording session, Karen, who idolised her brother, accompanied him and, through a series of misunderstandings, got to sing a ballad. Both Richard and Joe were transfixed, and Carpenters biographer Ray Coleman identifies this chance occasion as the moment when Richard first realised that his sister had a sensational voice. Osborn became friendly with Richard and Karen, and offered Karen the opportunity to make her own record, which would be released on his own Magic Lamp label. A single was released (and was later included on the retrospective *From The Top* Carpenters boxed set), but it flopped, as Magic Lamp lacked the resources to promote it, and the label folded shortly after the single appeared.

Following the RCA disappointment Wes Jacobs went to the Juilliard Music School and the trio disbanded. Richard Carpenter then teamed up with John Bettis, a university friend who performed as a folk singer, to form Spectrum, a vocal harmony group which included Karen on drums and vocals; guitarist Gary Sims and bassist Danny Woodhams (both of whom would became firmly-established members of the backing band behind The Carpenters); and another female vocalist, Leslie Johnston. However, although the group's *sound* was more acceptable and more in step with the times, Spectrum did not look like hip young gunslingers, and once again their efforts were rejected by the record industry - even 30 years ago (long before MTV), an appropriate visual image was regarded as vital for success.

During the summer of 1967, Richard Carpenter and John Bettis worked as a banjo (Bettis) and piano entertainment duo at Disneyland There was little opportunity for them to play their own music, as they were required to play familiar songs for the visitors who flocked to the place deservedly regarded as an Eighth Wonder Of The World, but it was this period of their lives which inspired the duo to write the first Carpenters single, 'Your Wonderful Parade'.

After Spectrum had been rejected by

two prominent labels, Bettis left the group (although he continued to write songs with Richard Carpenter). Soon afterwards, Spectrum broke up, and Richard & Karen continued with another bass player, and appeared several times on television. Destiny struck when their manager, Ed Sulzer, found his way to Herb Alpert, the trumpet-playing leader of The Tijuana Brass, a group who had taken five LPs to the top of the *Billboard* album chart between 1965 and 1968, and who had launched his own influential label, A&M Records, with his partner, Jerry Moss.

Alpert recalls the first time he heard The Carpenters: "I heard a tape around 1969, and I heard about them from the guitar player that used to play with The Tijuana Brass, John Pisano - his friend said 'I've got a group that Herb should hear', so he let me have a tape. To start with I was really knocked out with the sound of Karen's voice. Then when I realised that they had made all the sounds on the tape: Karen was playing drums, they were singing all the backgrounds, Richard in addition to playing the piano was also playing all the percussion parts and had developed the sound - it touched me. It had nothing to do with what was happening in the market at that moment, but that's what touched me even more, I felt like it was time."

While the comparison may appear bizarre, a similar, if more deliberately planned, approach was taken by Malcolm McLaren when he launched The Sex Pistols at a time when their outrageous behaviour and limited musical skills ran contrary to perceived public taste. The Carpenters were light years away from heavy metal, psychedelia and the drug culture, but - like McLaren - Alpert sensed that the musical tide would turn before long, and that a diametrically opposite approach would be seen as a total contrast, a refreshing change. Jerry Moss could see his partner's point: "I believe the first time I heard their voices was a tape that Herb played for me one day, and he told me he was going to have them perform on our soundstage because he was really excited about this group, and wanted to make a point that he was so proud of their signing. He was in love with their sound and, in particular Karen's voice and what he heard as far as the arrangements that Richard was preparing. I mean, the demo tape said a lot: they had played around as a band and they were experienced for their age, certainly for that genre of music. He was quite taken with it."

Shortly before Herb Alpert heard that tape, an opportunity had arisen for Karen which, like the Magic Lamp episode, promised much, but ultimately produced disappointment. One of the most popular acts of the time was Kenny Rogers & The First Edition, who had enjoyed a US Top Five hit with the curiously titled 'Just Dropped In (To See What Condition My Condition Was In)'. One of their singers, Thelma Camaco, was leaving the group, and a new female vocalist was required. Karen auditioned at Richard's urging, but failed the test. Not long after this, Herb Alpert signed The Carpenters, and their recording career began.

Acknowledgments

This book is a labour of love, whose author wishes to gratefully acknowledge assistance from the following: Marilyn Botheras (for her encyclopaedic knowledge and her trust); Andrew Doe (for his research and his initial draft); Lynda Morrison (for research, enthusiasm, proof reading, gardening, etc.); Cyriel van den Hemel (for permission to use quotes from filmed interviews conducted by the author for a TV documentary on The Carpenters which we would still like to complete); Herb Alpert, Burt Bacharach, John Bettis, Richard Carpenter, Jerry Moss, Tony Peluso and Paul Williams. All quotes are copyright Cyriel van den Hemel and John Tobler.

Thanks also to Chris and Henrietta (which is a very good name, and one to be proud of) at Omnibus, and condolences to anyone who still thinks The Carpenters were not rock superstars - a visit to a taxidermist is recommended.

This book is respectfully dedicated to Karen Carpenter, Ray Coleman and Thomas Gray, all sadly no longer with us, and to my mother, my children (including Jay), my grandchildren and my extended family.

John Tobler, August 1997

CARPENTERS
TICKET TO RIDE

STEREO

AMLS 64205

Offering

A&M SP-4205; RELEASED IN 1969, RERELEASED AS TICKET TO RIDE; UK: A&M AMLS 64342.

Accounting to Richard Carpenter's notes in the Compact Disc Collection boxed set, The Carpenters signed with A&M in April 1969, and began recording their début LP almost immediately. He calls the album "definitely a reflection of its time", and adds that he "shudders" to think of the picture on the sleeve of himself and Karen. As *Offering,* the album failed to chart, but after 'Ticket To Ride' became a minor US hit single, and was followed by the considerable success of '(They Long To Be) Close To You' (a million selling chart-topper) and the equally impressive performance of the *Close To You* LP, it was repackaged and reissued and (under the title *Ticket To Ride)* spent four months in the Billboard album chart in early 1971, although it has always been regarded as little more than the first faltering step on the ladder to fame.

With only 25 per cent of the material from outside sources, and with a style of music that was the absolute antithesis of the prevailing musical trends, it would have been a miracle if the album had been a success first time round. The sleeve bore the crdit "Produced by Jack Daugherty" (apparently he introduced Ed Sulzer to A&M), but Richard has always maintained that, to all intents and purposes, he produced the album himself.

INVOCATION
(Carpenter/Bettis)

This lush introduction to *Offering* was, according to Richard, written with the intention of having "some fun overdubbing in the a cappella vein". The album version is a near carbon-copy re-recording of a song first cut in Joe Osborn's garage studio in 1968, before The Carpenters had a recording contract. The original recording (spot the difference!) appears on the *From The Top* four CD set.

YOUR WONDERFUL PARADE
(Carpenter/Bettis)

Bearing in mind that The Carpenters were regarded as bastions of "The Establishment" from the very earliest days of their career, the lyric (by John Bettis) of this snare drum and harpsichord-driven number comes across as something dangerously close to subversive. Written in 1967, and another product of the Osborn garage sessions, the original version was included on the demo tape sent to Herb Alpert, and also appears on the *From The Top* set in a form lacking both Richard's cynical circus-style spoken intro and the decidedly unwise phasing of the drum outro. This track, according to Bettis, was the original A-side of the (unsuccessful) very first Carpenters single, but was later relegated to the B-side of 'Ticket To Ride' which was a minor US hit, peaking just outside the Top 50. The original version of 'Your Wonderful Parade' forms the basis

of this recording. The four-track tape from the Osborn session was transferred to A&M's eight-track machine, enabling Richard's lead vocal to be re-recorded, and a string section added to the existing bass, drums, piano and backing vocals.

SOMEDAY
(Carpenter/Bettis)

Karen was reportedly never happy with her vocal performance of this poignant ballad, but a far greater problem with this track is the melodramatic orchestral arrangement, which at times threatens to swamp what is at heart a lovely composition. Karen later re-recorded a part of this song for a medley featured on the 1980 ABC-TV special, *Music, Music, Music*, which appears on *From The Top*.

GET TOGETHER
(Powers)

Previously a hit in late 1965 for We Five, a Californian vocal harmony quintet whose biggest success came earlier that year when 'You Were On My Mind' made the US Top Five, 'Get Together' is an archetypal hippie anthem. Chester Powers is widely believed to be a pseudonym adopted by Dino Valente, a true rock'n'roll gypsy whose major claim to fame (apart from this inspirational song) was his time as a member of San Francisco acid rock celebrities Quicksilver Messenger Service, with whom he recorded several highly-regarded albums in the early Seventies. 'Get Together' was also a minor US hit single in 1967 for The Youngbloods, a group from the East Coast of the USA who had migrated to San Francisco. In 1969, the single by The Youngbloods was reissued, sold a million copies and reached the US Top Five; apparently it was a big hit because it was adopted as the theme for the National Council Of Christians & Jews, an organisation which, purely on the strength of its name, must have been very hippie-credible.

The trends of the day dictated that Richard's verse vocals be heavily processed, thus providing an interesting contrast with the multi-tracked choruses.

The *From The Top* set included a live version, recorded in early 1970 for the *Your Navy Presents* radio show; this live reading differs most notably in that Karen takes the majority of the lead vocals (which are, of course, 'unprocessed').

ALL OF MY LIFE
(Carpenter)

Yet another track on the original Carpenters demo tape, this gentle song (written in 1967) could probably be regarded as the earliest example of the duo's trademark sound: a pleasantly restrained instrumental track, layered backing vocals and, of course, a warm lead vocal from Karen. Although Joe Osborn is credited on bass, some sources maintain that the bass player here is actually Karen, whom Osborn had taught the rudiments of the instrument.

TURN AWAY
(Carpenter/Bettis)

This sounds like something by Spanky And Our Gang - and is none the worse for that. The two-part structure of this song jostles for attention with the multi-part chorus vocals. Richard's lead vocal is less 'processed' here and sounds just fine.

TICKET TO RIDE
(Lennon/McCartney)

Richard's notion of rearranging The Beatles classic 1965 chart-topping single as a ballad was little short of inspired, as was Karen's rendering of the lead vocal. The first ever Carpenters hit single, it just failed to crack the US Top 50 despite a chart residency of many weeks.

When the compilation album, *The Singles* 1969 - 1973, was assembled, Karen chose to re-record both her vocal and the drums, while a guitar track was also added, and it is this revised version that appears on the *From The Top* set and probably all the many other compilation albums.

DON'T BE AFRAID
(Carpenter)

A delightfully upbeat track, with a lyric firmly rooted in the Sixties ("love is a groovy thing"). The original version of this song - another of the Osborn garage recordings from the demo tape - appears on the *From The Top* set.

WHAT'S THE USE
(Carpenter/Bettis)

Richard's voice finally appears in a totally unprocessed state on this mild yet perky ode to independence. A harpsichord adds a touch of class to an otherwise somewhat undistinguished item.

ALL I CAN DO
(Carpenter/Bettis)

Sporting a complex 5/4 time signature (best illustrated on Dave Brubeck's hit, 'Take Five'), and a vocal line that cuts across the rhythm, the composition of this title - a showcase for both Richard and Karen - dates back to 1967 and the Spectrum days. *From The Top* features the original Spectrum version, recorded initially as an instrumental in the Carpenter house.

EVE
(Carpenter/Bettis)

Inspired by an episode of a 1968 TV drama series, and thus suitably dramatic in its delivery and arrangement, this is another recording on which Karen reportedly provides the bass guitar as well as the drums.

NOWADAYS CLANCY CAN'T EVEN SING
(Young)

Just what Neil Young must have thought of this lush cover of the familiar Buffalo Springfield track isn't recorded, but for a pair of complete unknowns to attempt a radical reworking of such a classic shows considerable faith in their own abilities (and indicates the breadth of Richard's listening). Taken on its own terms, this is a perfectly acceptable track.

BENEDICTION
(Carpenter/Bettis)

Closing out the album just as 'Invocation' opened it, albeit with added strings.

CLOSE TO YOU
CARPENTERS

Close To You

A&M SP 4271; RELEASED AUGUST 1970; UK: AMLS 998; REISSUED DECEMBER 1990 AS CDA 3184

With *Offering* having made little impression, and with the general musical climate still favouring rock rather than pop, there was reportedly some surprise at A&M that the normally sure-footed Herb Alpert had not only retained The Carpenters on the label's roster, but had actually given them a second chance. Although he was the founder of a highly fashionable independent label whose roster included country/rock pioneers The Flying Burrito Brothers (a group whose leading lights were Chris Hillman & Gram Parsons, both ex-members of The Byrds), Alpert recognised that in the brother and sister, he had discovered an act with potentially massive appeal, and decided to allow them to make a second LP.

While 'Ticket To Ride' had been the track which had created most interest from *Offering*, it had made only a minor chart impact, but it had attracted the attention of a very significant and influential hitmaker and music industry professional. Burt Bachrach: "I was made aware of The Carpenters by the people at A&M Records, Jerry Moss & Herb Alpert in particular. I remember Herbie playing me a record that he had just done with them on the telephone; he played me 'Close To You', and I thought it was just a marvellous record. I had heard of them before, but I hadn't met them". 'Close To You' had been recorded by Dionne Warwick a few years before, but the version by The Carpenters had a very different arrangement (by Richard), of which Bacharach approved: "I loved it. When Herbie played it on the phone to me, I just thought it was an incredible sounding record, the definitive recording of that song." What Bacharach was unaware of at that time was that the favourite music of Richard & Karen Carpenter was what they called "the Three B's" -

The Beatles, The Beach Boys and Burt Bacharach - and when Bacharach suggested to Herb Alpert that the still little-known duo, whom he had never met, should be his opening act for a charity show, The Carpenters could hardly believe their luck. Bacharach also suggested that he would like to hear them perform a medley of songs written by himself and lyricist Hal David.

Alpert recalls: "I was doing some work with Burt Bacharach & Hal David, and Hal David mentioned to me this song that was recorded years back with Dionne Warwick that he really thought would be great for The Carpenters, and that was 'Close To You', so I pesented that song to Richard. There was a whole sequence of events and they recorded it three times. The first time, I didn't feel like the recording was what it wanted to be, the second time it was a little bit closer, and the third time was the charm, and that was obviously the breakthrough record for them".

Another version of this story suggests that Bacharach had suggested 'Close To You' as a follow-up to Alpert's 1968 chart-topping single, 'This Guy's In Love With You', which was his first big hit as a vocalist (as opposed to a trumpeter), and which was also written by Bacharach & David, but that Alpert decided that the song's lyrics were too unsophisticated for him to deliver credibly. However, he had remembered the song, and because it was not well-known beside the string of Bacharach/David compositions which made Dionne Warwick a star, suggested that Richard work out an arrangement of it to perform as part of the medley. According to a very reliable source, Bacharach insisted that the twiddly piano motif was retained, but this was his only stipulation. It was the first million-selling Number One single for The Carpenters, and it started a month-long residency at the top during which time the album was released. It couldn't fail - and it didn't.

WE'VE ONLY JUST BEGUN

(Williams/Nichols)

Songwriter Paul Williams: "'We've Only Just Begun' had the romantic beginnings of a bank commercial for the Crocker Bank. It was a new kind of commercial - they were going to show a young couple getting married and riding off into the sunset. The copy was written - 'You've got a long way to go and we'd like to help you get there. The Crocker Bank', and they said 'Write us a song', so Roger and I wrote the first two verses of 'We've Only Just Begun', and I sang it. My voice is evidently pretty recognisable - it's not a favourite of mine (now), but it was then: in those days I loved the way I sang - and Richard Carpenter heard it. He said 'Is there a full version of it ?', and I said 'Funny you should ask, you know', because we'd written a full version of it, and there was a record just coming in the charts by Mark Lindsay of 'We've Only Just Begun' that was eclipsed by The Carpenters. It's been the most amazing experience I've ever had in songwriting, because it became a wedding song. When Karen sang my lyrics, there was a purity there that was also sensual for me, just very sensual in a very clean way, like good clean sex, I suppose... And people related to it, they related to the way she sang the song. 'We've Only Just Begun' pretty much became the wedding song, the new contemporary wedding song - it was a great gift I got from Karen & Richard beyond just having a hit, something that kind of stuck in people, it got stuck in their year books, it got stuck in their family history. It's a wonderful thing about The Carpenters in general that so many times I've found parents coming to me and saying 'I finally found something I can enjoy with my children', and on the other side, teenagers coming to me and saying 'You know I like The Carpenters, and so do my folks'. It kind of brought them together. Something that had fallen off totally in the world of music was sheet music sales. If a song was a hit right now, I suppose a piece of sheet music of a hit song, a Number One record, might sell

30 - 50,000 copies. I'm told we've sold over 3 million copies of sheet music to 'We've Only Just Begun', and what that means is that people are learning to play it, and it means that the music is alive in their homes, and that's a real nice feeling." This was one of the earliest examples of a song written expressly for a television commercial becoming a hit record (as opposed to old hits being used in TV commercials and becoming hits again as a result). Richard first came across the song as a one minute advert for the Crocker Citizens Bank of California, and was so taken that he had to find out if there was more to the song. Luckily for him, Williams and collaborator Roger Nichols were staff writers at A&M, which made his task considerably simpler. Released as a single concurrently with the *Close To You* album, 'We've Only Just Begun' also sold a million copies, only just failing to top the US chart (which would have made two Number Ones in three months !) and nestled comfortably in the UK Top 30.

The advances in both recording, performance and arrangement over the first album are astonishing, a finely balanced production making this a template for almost all future Carpenters hits: Karen's yearning vocal backed by a restrained string arrangement and, of course, sumptuous harmonies. This has become their signature tune, and was always used to "top and tail" Carpenters TV Specials.

LOVE IS SURRENDER
(Carmichael)

Clocking in at just under two minutes, this sprightly little item - originally a contemporary religious song - shuffles along with great good humour, boasting an electric piano riff not a million miles removed from 'Do You Know The Way To San Jose?', and allowing Richard to share the vocal chores with Karen. There is something special about this track which is hard to put into words, and it might qualify as one of the undiscovered gems of the recorded repertoire of The Carpenters. The track crossfades into...

MAYBE IT'S YOU
(Carpenter/Bettis)

Dipping once more into the rapidly dwindling stockpile of pre-Carpenters compositions (this song dates from the 1968 and Spectrum days) enabled Richard to complete *Close To You* without having to compose in the studio (always the last resort of a desperate musician). The result was an album highlight, perhaps marginally marred by a slightly overbusy orchestral arrangement, but redeemed by the vocals, both lead and backing. Here, as elsewhere on the album, the drums are handled by stellar sessioneer Hal Blaine - if it was a hit recorded in Los Angeles in the Sixties and Seventies, chances are Blaine played on it, be it the Beach Boys, Glen Campbell or John Denver.

REASON TO BELIEVE
(Hardin)

Tim Hardin's classic (later covered by Rod Stewart and any number of country artists) is given an early country make-over here, highlighted by Karen's somewhat mournful reading. This was considered as a possible single: Richard & Karen had been performing this song ever since the mid-Sixties.

HELP
(Lennon/McCartney)

Richard's unorthodox harpsichord-based rearrangement of The Beatles' classic, coupled with precisely enunciated lyrics make for a somewhat atypical Carpenters recording that is nonetheless compelling and ultimately satisfying. Until the next track came along, 'Help' was slated to be The Carpenters second single release.

(THEY LONG TO BE) CLOSE TO YOU
(David/Bacharach)

On this song's release, Richard was unsure of its commercial potential, stating it would either make Number One - or flop totally. A good prediction - four weeks in pole position in the US, while in the UK, the single reached the Top

Ten. This was apparently the first Carpenters studio recording to feature Hal Blaine on drums rather than Karen (adding more muscle and allowing Karen to concentrate on her vocals), and the trumpet part, though very much in the style of Herb Alpert, is actually by Chuck Findley. Nominated for five Grammy awards, this track won two.

BABY IT'S YOU
(David/Bacharach/Williams)

A wistfully atmospheric cover of another composition of some vintage (originally a Top Ten hit in 1962 for New Jersey girl group The Shirelles, and included on the chart-topping *Please Please Me* debut LP by The Beatles) further showcases the emerging Carpenters blueprint. The Williams credited as one of the songwriters wasn't Paul, by the way, and the other two co-writers are not Hal & Burt, but Hal's brother, Mack David, and Burt.

I'LL NEVER FALL IN LOVE AGAIN
(Bacharach/David)

A US Top Ten hit for Dionne Warwick in early 1970 (before the release of the *Close To You* album), this pleasantly undemanding cover would appear to have been arranged by Richard in a sub-Bacharach style. The song was part of the score of *Promises, Promises*, a theatrical musical written by Bacharach & David in 1968. Although the Dionne Warwick version failed to make any chart headway in Britain, it was a 1969 UK Number One hit for Bobbie 'Ode To Billie Joe' Gentry. The song is also featured as part of the Bacharach/David medley which appears on the *Carpenters* album

CRESCENT NOON
(Carpenter/Bettis)

One of the four songs on this album dating back to the Spectrum days, and perhaps showing its age a little, the stately chord progression used by Richard suggests that it was strongly influenced by Erik Satie, the 20th century French composer best known for the *Trois Gymnopedies* pieces. The string arrangement is nicely understated, and Karen is in sterling vocal form. The title of this song is often mis-spelt as

'Crescent Moon', for example, on the 12xCD boxed set. There are also reports that the sound of the drum beat here made many fans exchange copies of the album which they mistakenly presumed were scratched.

MR. GUDER
(Carpenter/Bettis)

The summer vacation of 1967 found Richard and John Bettis performing at Coke Corner on Main Street USA in Disneyland, cranking out turn of the century hits to keep the crowds amused between rides... and to relieve the tedium, the duo occasionally tossed in the odd current hit, to the irritation of their boss, one Victor Guder, whom they lampooned in this perky little number, which became a concert favourite.

John Bettis: "He was our supervisor at 'the park' as they call it, and when you work at Disneyland - I don't know how it is today, but in those days they had very strict regimens as to what one could and could not do in the park, and Richard and I were fired for combing our

hair in the park. 'Mr Guder' was a song that we wrote after we were fired from Disneyland, really written out of anger at the whole thing he represented to us."

Richard Carpenter: "Looking back, it's a bit harsh, really. At the time it was popular to deride the establishment. Our generation, which has become an establishment of its own, wasn't going to be a member of the establishment, and to me and to John, he kind of personified the whole thing. We didn't do as we were told. We would perform modern day tunes when we were supposed to be doing tunes from the turn of the century. We were a little rebellious and were finally fired, and we wrote this song. But now that the years have gone by and I'm looking back at this, it really wasn't a very nice thing to do because the man was just doing his job. It's got a number of different time signatures, it's mildly jazzy, and I think it was a mixture of everything I was listening to at the time. We were in the choir at Cal State U (California State University) at Long Beach, so it's got the choral section. I was listening to Lalo Schifrin and Dave Brubeck and so it's got some of the jazz influences. I was majoring in piano and studying the classics, so it's got some classical influences. It's actually quite an interesting piece. I like it."

I KEPT ON LOVING YOU
(Williams/Nichols)

Songwriter Paul Williams: "My relationship with The Carpenters actually goes back before 'We've Only Just Begun' to when Jack Daugherty brought The Carpenters to A&M. Even though Roger Nichols and I, who were writing together at the time, had never really had any hits, they [The Carpenters] had an amazing awareness of our music, and I think a lot of it was through Roger's group, A Small Circle Of Friends - they were fans already. The first sessions [for the *Close To You* album] included a song I wrote called 'I Kept On Loving You', which I don't think would have been a hit if it had been released as a single, which was what we were hoping for. They wanted it on the back of 'Close To You', which was their first hit, so I got the traditional free ride that every songwriter dreams of. 'Close To You' was the A-side and the B-side was 'I Kept On Loving You', and we were getting paid anyway!".

For a change, Richard is the featured vocalist on this thoroughly good-natured item, a song that couldn't hail from any other era, sounding as though it belongs over the opening credits of a TV movie. Splendid fluff.

ANOTHER SONG
(Carpenter/Bettis)

Yet another Spectrum-era composition (the inclusion of so many would seem to indicate a lack of ready material for the album), the multi-part construction and lengthy instrumental passage tends to distract rather than intrigue, and again it's Karen's voice that stays in the memory once the self-consciously 'clever' track ends.

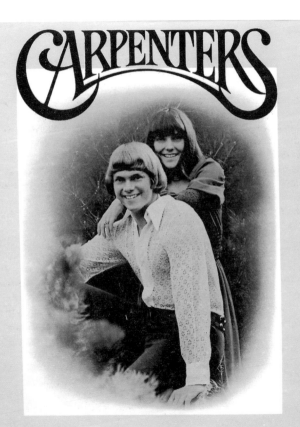

CARPENTERS

A&M RECORDS

AMLS 63502

Carpenters

A&M SP-3502; RELEASED IN MAY 1971: UK: AMLS 63502; REISSUED IN DECEMBER 1990 AS CDA 3502

With a gold album under their belts (and a belated chart US appearance for *Offering*, now retitled *Ticket To Ride*) plus a couple of million-selling singles, this third LP could hardly fail. With 'For All We Know' previewing the album by becoming the duo's third US Top Three single in nine months, as well as two more US Top Three singles which also sold a million copies to follow, Carpenters is regarded as the best original LP by Richard & Karen, although most fans apparently prefer *Close To You* (which remained many months longer in the US album chart), or *A Song For You*, while younger fans seemingly like *Made In America* best. *Carpenters* again credits Jack Daugherty as producer.

RAINY DAYS AND MON-DAYS
(Williams/Nichols)

Paul Williams: "The next Carpenters hit we had was 'Rainy Days And Mondays'. I didn't go into the studio with them; they weren't looking over my shoulder when I was writing the lyrics, so I didn't look over their shoulder when they were recording. So it was always a surprise for me - when they would play something for me, it was usually pretty well done. And I loved the record of 'We've Only Just Begun', but the record of 'Rainy Days And Mondays' I liked much much more. There was something, I don't know if it was the saxophone [played by Bob Messenger, a longtime member of the touring and studio band who backed The Carpenters], or what it was, but it sounded awfully grown up for something that I'd been involved with. And I don't know, there was something about her that was... I guess I had a crush on her, now that I think about it. When you hear that lady sing those words you've got to know there was a little bit of a connection there. I remember her playing at the rehearsal hall and soundstage at A&M, playing me the record and watching me listening to it, and it was a real pretty memory... I was very young then, of course."

Another gem from the pen(s) of Paul Williams and Roger Nichols, this wonderfully introspective ballad was submitted along with many other demos and caught Richard's ear after just two plays. Tommy Morgan's plaintive harmonica introduction sets the tone of a song that, released as a single, just missed the number one spot in the US.

SATURDAY
(Carpenter/Bettis)

A splendid - if concise - showcase for both Richard's vocal and spirited brother and sister harmonies, this chirpy little tune (or at least the chorus), which was written in 1967, has subsequently graced many a weekend radio program.

LET ME BE THE ONE
(Williams/Nichols)

This classic number emerged from the same demo pile as 'Rainy Days And Mondays', and could be considered a companion piece to that song. The version featured on *From The Top* includes a tiny fragment of Karen practising the vocal over the count-in - and singing that she has forgotten the lyrics! Paul Williams: "You know, neither 'I Won't Last A Day Without You' nor 'Let Me Be The One' by The Carpenters were really hits, and yet they had such a high recognisability because of the fact that they were on the *Carpenters* album."

(A PLACE TO) HIDEAWAY
(Sparks)

One of Spectrum's few bookings was at a club owned by one Randy Sparks, formerly of The New Christy Minstrels, and Richard always remembered Randy performing this song that night. The yearning ballad fits in perfectly among the others on this album.

FOR ALL WE KNOW
(Karlin/Wilson/James)

Following the phenomenal success of both '(They Long To Be) Close To You' and 'We've Only Just Begun', the problem of finding something to continue the run of hit singles began weighing on Richard's mind. While The Carpenters were on tour in Canada in late 1970 (opening for Engelbert Humperdinck), their manager Sherwin Bash suggested they see a movie called *Lovers And Other Strangers*, which featured 'For All We Know': problem solved. Released in early 1971, the single stopped just short of the US Number One position, and, for good measure, cracked the UK Top 30. Introduced by Earl Dumler's oboe (an instrument set to become something of a Carpenters trademark) and sporting gorgeous block harmonies, this became the band's third million-selling 45 out of four releases - not a bad strike rate! The movie version of the song later won the Academy Award for Best Song of 1970. Interestingly, the James who co-wrote the song was actually James Griffin, and the Wilson was Rob Wilson, both of whom were founder members of Bread.

SUPERSTAR
(Russell/Bramlett)

Richard Carpenter: "I wind down by watching TV, and I'd come home from recording one night and turned on the Johnny Carson Show. He would have Bette Midler (as a) guest quite often, and this was before she was a household name, and on this particular appearance, she sang 'Superstar'. And she sang it more as kind of a modern day torch song, but the song really caught my ear. I thought it was a hit, no two ways about it. There's some that grow on me, and others where I'm kind of on the fence as to whether I think they are or they aren't, but 'Superstar', I really thought it had it all. So we cut it, and it was one of the very few tunes that Karen ever questioned me on. Usually, our tastes were exactly the same and I thought she'd just go crazy over this, and she didn't. So I asked her to just indulge me and sing it and listen to the record as it was being put together, and she changed her mind, it became one of her favourites. It's a perfect song for Karen. It's a haunting melody, it's a great hook, Bonnie Bramlett's lyric is definitely a little off the beaten path, and just as far as the vowel sounds and all, radio and away and all, it worked so perfectly for Karen. We did change one word, in the second verse: 'I can hardly wait to sleep with you again', we thought was just a little bit too much for The Carpenters and their listening audience, so we changed it to 'Be with you again'. But that remains one of my favourite Carpenters recordings". Amazingly, Karen's vocal was a "work lead", designed as a run through, but it was so good there was no need to record it again."

Even after recording the track, Richard was torn between 'Superstar' and 'Let Me Be The One' as the next single. Jerry Moss swayed his decision, and the single emulated 'For All We Know' in the chart stakes Stateside, while making the Top 20 in the UK. The subject matter - basically a groupie's lament for a rock musician - was light years away from the perceived image of The Carpenters at the time, even after Richard's lyrical revision, and it's a tribute to Karen's haunting rendition that a song already well known from Rita Coolidge's then current album version could chart so high. Co-composer Leon Russell was another of the cream of the West Coast session musicians (on keyboards) and was just breaking out into solo stardom at this time.

DRUSCILLA PENNY
(Carpenter/Bettis)

By a quirk of sequencing (or maybe not!), 'Superstar' was followed by Richard's comprehensive put-down of groupies - perhaps he felt a need to reassure The Carpenters' audience that all was as it should be. Driven along briskly by harpsichord and bass and featuring Richard's own vocal this is definitely a period piece.

ONE LOVE
(Carpenter/Bettis)

Originally entitled 'Candy', this is another of the pre-Carpenters compositions, inspired by a waitress at Disneyland who caught their fancies. A sweet and inoffensive ballad.

BACHARACH/DAVID MEDLEY

Knowing When To Leave/Make It Easy On Yourself/(There's) Always Something There To Remind Me/I'll Never Fall In Love Again/Walk On By/Do You Know The Way to San Jose?
(Bacharach/David)

Could this be the medley The Carpenters performed at Burt Bacharach's 1970 charity show? Very nearly - the original medley kicked off with two other titles, 'Any Day Now' and 'Baby It's You', and Richard always regretted trimming it down for this album (for details of the full medley, see the *Anthology* compilation). Also, it doesn't include 'Close To You', while all the titles are songs recorded by Dionne Warwick, for whom Bacharach & David produced 39 US hit singles between 1972 and 1982, the vast majority songs they had also written. Medleys have a tendency to diminish the individual elements, but here the strength of both the material and performance overcomes any such fears. Perhaps surprisingly, there seems never to have been a *Carpenters Sing Bacharach & David* album... now wouldn't that have been splendid ?

SOMETIMES
(Mancini/Mancini)

A beautifully understated piano & vocal number completes the album. Composed by Henry Mancini (of *Pink Panther* fame), who set a poem by his daughter Felice to music, this utterly lovely ballad features Richard's piano and Karen's voice in equal proportion. They were walking past one of the recording studios at A&M when they heard Mancini playing it, and as they liked it, they decided to record it. There is a theory that Richard & Karen recorded this song as a tribute to their parents.

A Song For You

A&M SP-3511; RELEASED IN 1972; UK: AMLS 63511; REISSUED IN DECEMBER 1990 AS CDA 3511

By the time this fourth Carpenters LP was released, Richard & Karen were flying high: in less than two years, they had two gold albums and five gold singles under their collective belts, and everything was looking very positive, a situation consolidated by *A Song For You* becoming their third gold album in two years, and giving them (eventually) six US Top 20 singles, including their second Number One.

A SONG FOR YOU
(Russell)

The title track, another Leon Russell composition (from his eponymous début solo album), takes the seasoned and successful Carpenters recipe and ices it with a sultry sax break by Bob Messenger, enhanced by a sparse production, for a splendid album opener which many felt could have been a single, had the album not already contained a plethora of hits.

TOP OF THE WORLD
(Carpenter/Bettis)

The author confesses that it was hearing this on the Los Angeles radio while uncertainly cruising the freeways that first alerted him to the discovery that The Carpenters were clearly not the wimps which the UK music press had suggested but were in tune with musical fashion, and were capable of perfect pop music. The problem was that they looked wrong at a time when UK record buyers were adoring a largely average bunch of teenybop acts...

A country song with steel guitar? Richard Carpenter: "Well every now and again we used steel guitar because I thought it worked so well for Karen's voice. We'd used it on earlier things we did, and I should have used it in 'Reason

To Believe' but I didn't think of it at the time. 'Top Of The World' has quite an interesting story surrounding it. It's odd. It was written by one kid from San Pedro (Bettis) and another one from Downey and it's a country song, but when we finished it for the *A Song For You* album in 1972, all of us thought 'It's an album cut', and we were proved so wrong, for a number of reasons. Firstly, when we performed it in concert, it got an ovation from the crowd as if it were one of our biggest hits. The Japanese culled it from the LP and released it as a single and it went gold. Lynn Anderson covered it, almost to the note, and it went to Number One in the country chart. Certain stations in the United States were charting it, based on requests alone. We had kids coming to our parents' home asking when it was going to be made into a small record. So we decided it was time to release it as a single. A & M wasn't all that happy about putting it out, so they kind of talked us out of it. Time went by and it just didn't let up, the requests for it and all, and we ultimately did a little alteration to it. We redid the lead, because Karen thought she could sing it better, and I was never totally happy with the steel guitar on the album. So we did the steel guitar over and then Tony (Peluso) came in and did a little guitar work on it, and then we remixed it. And, of course, it went to Number One in all three trade papers in the States and it was a smash."

It's comforting to know that Richard's musical ear isn't 100 per cent infallible. Not only did the single top the US charts, it also reached the Top Five in Britain. The album version (included on *From The Top*) featured O.J. "Red" Rhodes on steel guitar, while the single mix (which appears on all other compilations) had Buddy Emmons taking over on steel, Tony Peluso on guitar, a general remix and the new lead vocal from Karen.

HURTING EACH OTHER
(Udell/Geld)

This was the first 'taster' from the new LP (other than 'Bless The Beasts & Children', which was written specifically for a film), and was released as a single in January, 1972, when it became the sixth gold single for The Carpenters in just over 18 months. Richard Carpenter: "Bob Udell and Gary Geld had written 'Save Your Heart For Me', (which was a US Top Three hit for) Gary Lewis & The Playboys. 'Hurting Each Other' was released, I believe, in 1969, or right around there, on A&M Records by none other than Ruby & The Romantics, who'd had a Number One record in 1963 with 'Our Day Will Come'; and the treatment of it was quite a bit like 'Our Day Will Come'. The verses were done in the bossa nova fashion and then it went into the straight rock ballad, or rhythm ballad, feel for the hooks. I heard it on an LA radio station several times, and I was convinced it was a hit. I remember, because A&M was going through a bit of a drought at the time with single hits, and I thought 'This is gonna be the one that's going to do it. And I was wrong. It wasn't a hit. It really wasn't a hit. I couldn't figure it out, I can't figure it out to this day, but I never

forgot the song, and come 1971, I did a different treatment of it and, to me, one of my better arrangements. I am really happy with that record and it became our sixth gold single."

IT'S GOING TO TAKE SOME TIME
(King/Stern)

As a follow-up to 'Hurting Each Other', this Carole King/Toni Stern number, released just before the album, was a relative disappointment in chart terms as it was (apart from 'Bless The Beasts') their first single since 'Ticket To Ride' to peak outside the US Top Three, and in fact peaked just outside the US Top Ten.

Richard Carpenter: "Being a student of the business, I was very familiar with Carole King & Gerry Goffin (her first husband). They'd written so many melodic, timeless tunes, and we'd met her. She was with Ode Records that was distributed by A&M and she was recording *Tapestry* in the studios at the same time we were doing the

Carpenters album. A year later, she was working on the *Music* album and I heard 'It's Going To Take Some Time This Time', which to me is a little bit different from a lot of Carole's tunes. It's not as knock'em dead commercial pop Carole King as, say, 'Will You Still Love Me Tomorrow', or some of the others, but it's a classy little tune and I liked it and we recorded it. It wasn't one of our bigger singles, but I like the record to this day. It's odd, once I heard it on the radio, I knew it wasn't gonna be that big a hit. Wish I'd known this a little before, but I had to hear it in context with everything else that was out at the time. I was in Baltimore when I heard it on the radio, and thought 'Mmm, I like it, but it's not going Top Five', and it didn't."

Richard apparently heard the song when a new hi-fi system was being installed at the Carpenter home, and the installer used the Carole King album to test the new system - Richard was reportedly struck by the song, and decided to record it.

GOODBYE TO LOVE
(Carpenter/Bettis)

This was the first hit single written by the Carpenter/Bettis team, as Richard recalled: "'Goodbye To Love' is more revered in the UK than it is in the United States. It was a US Top Ten hit, but people think more of it here than in the United States. Part of it was written in 1971, when we were on the continent (of Europe) and in the UK doing promotions. I came up with the idea for the song after having watched an old Bing Crosby film called *Rhythm Of The River*, and in it, Bing plays a ghost writer for a well-known songwriter whose best known song is 'Goodbye To Love'. In the film, you never hear 'Goodbye To Love', it's just referred to, but I thought it was a great title for a song. I came up with the opening lyric, and my melody kept going and my lyrics stopped, because I'm not a lyricist. I'd come up with that much of it while I was over here, and then I completed it upon our return, and I called John (Bettis) to finish the lyric."

John Bettis: "We had set aside some days to get together and write, because he was so busy touring and everything. We really had to make the most of our time, so we would have four or five days to write the songs for the next album, and he would be out on the road and I wouldn't see them until they were recording. I remember thinking that with 'Goodbye To Love' we broke through creatively, there was a freshness; better than a freshness: there was something about Richard training as a complete radio junkie and loving all the great hit records and also his training as a classical musician that kind of melted in that song and it was really pure. To be honest, I was very excited about that, and I was very nervous, because I was hoping that it would work. Then I would talk to him on the phone from time to time and he would say 'This new guy, Tony Peluso, wait till you hear his guitar solo !', and I was thinking 'Why is he going on about this guitar solo?'. And then when I got the record, I actually cried the first time I heard it, because I had never heard an electric guitar sound like that, and have very few times heard it sound that way since. Tony had a certain almost cello sounding guitar growl that worked against that wonderful melancholia of that song - the way it growls at you, especially at the end, is unbelievable. It's just a wonderful record."

Tony Peluso: "I joined Paul Revere & The Raiders, a popular American group at that time, and then Mark Lindsay, the lead singer of that group, struck out on his own and took me along with him and we formed a group called Instant Joy. The Carpenters were on to their third album and extremely successful at this point, the Grammy-winning Number One artists of America, and they took Mark Lindsay and our band, Instant Joy, on tour as the opening act. This was a great experience, I was a 20-year-old kid coming off the Sunset Strip hippie days and flung into these amazing arenas and concerts. The sound of The Carpenters was so unique and so wonderful, and Karen's voice - it takes several generations to come across a voice like that,

and to hear her every night and be a part of that just as the opening act, never mind later as a member of that group, was a thrill, it was tremendous. I got to know them pretty well: they were really nice folk, it wasn't like we were the opening act pushed off to one side and they were the stars that we would never have any contact with, they were great folks and we all joined together off-stage as well as on. During that tour, I noticed that when I would play solos during the show, Karen and Richard would be over in the wings watching me. I was pretty nervous about that, but then thrilled all at the same time that they would even take the time to watch, so I'd do an extra special job, of course, the best I could to impress them. I loved their music and their vocal sound so much, and I thought maybe someday we'd do something together, but never really thought that would happen, obviously. I was a long haired hippie freak and they were very clean cut, I liked loud blasting fuzztone rock'n'roll and they had a very smooth sound, and it was pretty obvious these two elements could never come together.

"About a year after that tour, I figured they had long since forgotten me, and I was home one night and I got a telephone call from Karen. I was quite taken aback - this was Karen Carpenter calling my home! And she said 'Tony, it's Karen Carpenter. What are you doing tonight?', and of course I said 'Nothing'. It wouldn't have mattered if I had an audience with The Pope, I think I would have said 'Nothing'. And she said 'Could you come over to the studio?' I lived very near by, as it happens, and I said 'Of course'. I didn't know what they wanted me to do, but I rushed over with my guitar. I was never more nervous before or since than that night, going over to their recording studio to do I didn't know what, to be involved in a record. Up to this point, the hit records that he had had, he had not penned: Roger Nichols & Paul Williams, Burt Bacharach, Hal David, and other writers had composed most of their hits - and Richard had written a very special song called 'Goodbye To Love';

it was quite a tour de force, with the choir ending, pipe organ, amazing vocal lines, and he wanted, I guess, a big finish and his call was for a Hendrix-type fuzz guitar solo. Looking back on it, I'm sure everybody thought he was nuts to even try such a thing, but he had the golden touch, and his finger was on the pulse of his public. So I am fortunate that by no, what should I say, vision of my own, and through his, I fell into the right place at the right time and played a solo. To make a long story short, that night I pulled out my guitar and plugged it into the board and after just a couple of takes, as memory serves me... we did that solo in a relatively short amount of time. It was meant to be, it was amazing how it worked. You would never have thought that their sound and this fuzz guitar solo would go together, and it seemed right instantly, it was really a magical moment for all of us in the studio... it was just overwhelming. I was up all night after I went home. I lived with my mother still, and I woke her up and told her all about it, and it was the greatest moment in my life to that point, and I was so excited. It went well from there, as you know, the solo is pretty well known. It's ironic that I've gone on to do seven or eight years with them after that and played on a lot of records, and had solos that I thought were much more professional and spot, but its the solo of 'Goodbye To Love' that seems to be what people want to remember. Of course, I'm proud that they remember anything at all. I'm grateful like heck to Richard and Karen for giving me that opportunity. He's good at that, he's good at taking people and situations and songs and putting them together and letting things happen - not really making them happen, but letting them happen, and so he gave me a great opportunity."

Richard: "We played him the song, and I said 'I want you to start by playing the melody, and then go crazy'. And he laid down, to me, one of the all time (great) recorded guitar solos. It's just an amazing solo. Three quarters of it was one take. We were so taken with this that we asked Tony to join our road group and he was with us really up until we disbanded, and he's played on many, many more of our records and today is a successful record producer and really doesn't play as much as he should, in my opinion."

Bizarrely, Richard Carpenter got some complaining letters, as John Bettis confirmed: "That was confusing to me. Once it had become a hit, I was extremely excited and so was Richard: it was really our first breakthrough single as writers. I remember saying 'Isn't it great, 'Goodbye To Love', isn't that a great record to hear on the air ?', and he said 'Yeah - I've got to tell you, it's strange, we're getting complaining letters on this, like 'The Carpenters have sold out', or 'What's this rock'n'roll guitar doing on a Carpenters record ?' Can you believe that ?', and I went 'No, I have no idea what they're talking about'. And I actually think it scared us for a minute, you know, because you don't want to bust the bubble but the record did well enough, I think, that we didn't worry about it too much after that."

Perhaps as a result of this mini-furore,

this third single release from the album - a chart-topper if ever there was one - stalled in the lower half of the Top Ten in both the US and the UK. It is worth considering that this song is also an awesome example of Karen's lung power, as she almost unbelievably sings two complete and very wordy lines unwaveringly with a single breath: "Time and time again the chance to love has passed me by, And all I know of love is how to live without it." Try it...

INTERMISSION
(Carpenter)

A fragment of heavenly harmony (with a small sting in the tail !), adapted by Richard from 'Crucifixus', a 17th/18th-century composition by an Italian named Antonio Lotti.

BLESS THE BEASTS AND THE CHILDREN
(De Vorzon/Botkin Jr.)

Like 'For All We Know' - although not exactly in the same class - this is a movie soundtrack item, this time one

The Carpenters were requested to record by Stanley Kramer, director of the film of the same title. It's a lovely, reflective song but, even though it garnered an Academy Award nomination, it somehow lacks the impact of 'For All We Know': possibly it worked better in the context of the movie.

FLAT BAROQUE
(Carpenter)

A charming and all too brief example of Richard's piano and arranging skills and Norm Herzberg's expertise on the bassoon, this track was first recorded during The Carpenters' brief (and unproductive) sojourn with RCA Records in 1966. It has been suggested that Richard's inspiration for this number was a 1966 album which laboured under the ludicrous title of *The Dissection And Reconstruction Of Music From The Past As Performed By The Inmates Of Lalo Schifrin's Demented Ensemble As A Tribute To The Memory Of The Marquis De Sade.*

PIANO PICKER
(Edelman)

An equally brief slice of apparent autobiography from Richard is actually from the pen of singer/songwriter Randy Edelman, who toured with The Carpenters in 1971, and is probably best known for writing Barry Manilow's 'Weekend In New England' and his own 1976 UK hit, 'Uptown Uptempo Woman' (perhaps inspired by his wife, "Pop Princess" Jackie De Shannon). Nevertheless, the lyric still fits Richard's character neatly enough, and it's all good fun.

I WON'T LAST A DAY WITHOUT YOU
(Williams/Nichols)

The reason why this song was issued as a single in the States nearly two years after the album was released (not to mention after the *Now And Then* LP) is a tale similar to that surrounding 'Top Of The World', i.e. public demand, which was justified not only by a chart position just outside the US Top Ten for this lush Williams & Nichols composition (and a UK chart ranking just outside the Top 30 for a song that had already charted high once before as a short-lived double A-side with 'Goodbye To Love') but also by it winning Japan's World Disc Grand Prix as single of the year for 1974.

CRYSTAL LULLABY
(Carpenter/Bettis)

A delicate instrumental track. The intriguing juxtaposition of Richard and Karen's vocals help to make this gently atmospheric Spectrum-era composition a hidden gem on an album of astonishingly high standards. Charming.

ROAD ODE
(Sims/Woodhams)

The unusual subject matter of the emptiness of the touring lifestyle would be somewhat at odds with the overall tone of the rest of the album were it not for the softening influence of a shimmering production and wistful arrangement. Bizarrely, the title of this song, which was written by the guitarist and bassist from The Carpenters tour band, Gary Sims and guitarist Danny Woodhams (neither of whom played on many Carpenters recordings), has been misspelled as 'Road One' on more than one reissue.

A SONG FOR YOU (REPRISE)
(Russell)

As the title indicates, a brief return for the opening track (not the first, nor the last, time that a Carpenters album would be "bookended" in this manner). Aside from heavy echo, this is exactly the same recording as before.

Now And Then

A&M SP-3519; RELEASED IN MAY 1973; UK: AMLS 63519; REISSUED IN DECEMBER 1990 AS CDA 3519

Still hugely popular, The Carpenters were almost certainly exhausted after releasing this, their fourth gold album in under three years, combined with a punishing touring schedule. The only Carpenter/Bettis composition on the album 'Yesterday Once More', was a million-selling hit, as was 'Sing' the LP's opening track. For many, the highlight of this album was the rock'n'roll/oldies medley, which was also an onstage highlight. The album was the third by The Carpenters to peak one position short of the very top, and was their last original LP to spend over six months in the Billboard chart.

SING
(Raposo)

If this slight yet perky little number sounds as though it escaped from a children's TV show... well, it did. Richard and Karen were appearing on a TV show entitled 'Robert Young And The Young', and 'Sing' - originally written for the long-running and deservedly hugely influential *Sesame Street* - was a featured song. Another song written by Raposo which appeared on an unlikely album was 'Green' (a lament by Kermit The Frog - "it's not easy being green") which appeared on Van Morrison's 1973 album, *Hard Nose The Highway*: Morrison said that he heard it when he was watching *Sesame Street* with his infant daughter, and liked the sentiment. Still smarting slightly from the criticism of 'Goodbye To Love' (and apparently against the advice of most of his friends), Richard decided to revert to formula, to such effect that the single release went Top Three in America and garnered two Grammy nomnations. The version included on *From The Top* features a combination of English and Spanish lyrics, the latter recorded by request. On both versions, the chorus is supplied by the Jimmy Joyce Children's

Choir, and as on all the tracks on *Now And Then*, Karen relieves Hal Blaine on the drum stool.

Richard Carpenter: "In early 1973, Karen and I were scheduled to do an ABC television special called *Robert Young With The Young*. It took just about a week's worth of rehearsals before the taping and we were guests along with Artie Johnson and Sandy Duncan, and it had a lot of children in it, obviously, and one of the tunes they were using was 'Sing', which was from *Sesame Street*. After five days of working on the special, that song was definitely under our collective skin. It's a very catchy and very well constructed tune, and I got the idea of getting a children's choir and making it one of our records. People either love it or hate it, there's no in-between with 'Sing' and the company did not want to release it. I stood my ground because I thought it was a nice record and a commercial one and this particular go round, I was right. It really surprised a lot of people at A&M: it went gold and it went to

Number Three in the United Sates and it still gets programmed a lot today. It's a song that lot of people still like."

THIS MASQUERADE
(Russell)

Karen's velvet tones are perfectly suited to what can only be described as a superior Seventies cocktail lounge music track, originally released on Leon Russell's *Carney* album. Bob Messenger's flute enhances the mood of what is a favourite track among Carpenters aficionados.

HEATHER
(Pearson)

Richard's delicate piano is the highlight of this atmospheric instrumental which is finely balanced just this side of melodramatic.

JAMBALAYA (ON THE BAYOU)
(Williams)

As a UK-only release, this jaunty, steel guitar and flute-propelled version of the Hank Williams country classic (previously a US Top 30 hit for Fats Domino in 1961) lodged comfortably in the Top 20 in early 1974. Probably the recent success of the similarly countryfied 'Top Of The World' precluded a US 45 issue, although in Japan it sold enough to be certified gold.

I CAN'T MAKE MUSIC
(Edelman)

Although this track was one which Edelman had performed while opening for The Carpenters on tour, and not one written specifically for them, its melodic introspection suited Karen's voice and lent itself well to Richard's wistfully yearning arrangement.

YESTERDAY ONCE MORE
(Carpenter/Bettis)

By the early Seventies, rock had begun to grow up, to have a history, and Richard chose to pay homage to this past with a song that was to include a verse comprised of the titles of oldies from the early Sixties. This notion was laid to rest as being basically unwork-able, but led to the subsequent track. The song celebrated the power of early Sixties AM radio and the warm feelings evoked by hearing those songs again many years down the line. As with many of the band's best items, there's more than a hint of nostalgia for a 'better' past, underlined by a suitably lush arrangement and production. Released as a single, 'Yesterday Once More' sold a million and just failed to top the charts on both sides of the Atlantic, becoming the eighth gold US Top Three single by The Carpenters in three years and giving them their best UK chart placing to date.

John Bettis: "I doubt that there is anyone alive who is the oldies fan that Richard is: also, the area of the country that he came from was very much more doo wop oriented than out here. I'm from L.A. and the whole doo wop thing was known here, but it wasn't anywhere near as common or as radio heavy as it was back East. Richard actually educated me to a lot of records that I had kind of overlooked - he educated me into an oldies aficionado. You can't be around him and not know two things, old records and cars, those are the two things that you learn with Richard. The funniest thing about that was the chorus: 'every sha la la la, every wo wo wo' was kind of a dummy lyric that we were singing along, expecting at some point we would lift that and put real words in there, and Richard was kind of surprised. We'd finished the song and he said 'Well, are you going to change this now?' and I went 'You know what? I don't think so, I think it sounds great this way', and he said 'Are you kidding?' I said 'No, this sha la la wo wo wo stuff sounds pretty good', and I think he had to think about that for a day or two before he really said 'OK'. It's a perfect play in to that era of music, I think."

OLDIES MEDLEY

Fun, Fun, Fun (Wilson/Love)/The End Of The World (Dee/Kent)/Da Doo Ron Ron (Barry/Greenwich/Spector)/Dead Man's Curve (Berry/Christian/Kornfeld /Wilson)/Johnny Angel (Pockriss/Duddy) / The Night Has A Thousand Eyes

(Weisman/Wayne/Garrett)/ Our Day Will Come (Garson/Hilliard) /One Fine Day (King/Goffin)

Richard Carpenter: "The 'Now & Then' side two medley took a great deal of research: one reason for 'Fun Fun Fun' was because right from the outset I knew I wanted a song to set up the medley, and of course that became 'Yesterday Once More', but out of the fade of 'Yesterday Once More', I wanted the car revving and panning drag strip sound, a race sound, and in all honesty there are other early Beach Boy tunes that I like far more than 'Fun Fun Fun', like 'I Get Around', but I don't know that the car revving would have been the same. We could have done 'Little Honda' but then you would have needed a motorcycle and it wasn't the same, so I thought 'Fun Fun Fun' was the one to use. 1963, to me, was one of the top two years for modern popular music, the other being 1964. That was a time when a person could turn on the radio and not have to be bopping from station to station. It was just one great piece after another, and one of these was Skeeter Davis's 'The End Of The World', which I never ever get tired of, and believe me, I've heard it plenty. A perfect song for Karen. When we moved to Downey in 1963, we ended up in a local talent show. Not a contest, just a show in one of the local parks. And I went up and played the 'Theme From Exodus' and I asked Karen to come up too; she was 13, and in her high voice - she hadn't developed the great low one - she sang 'The End Of The World'. So I definitely wanted to include it in this medley."

Kentucky-born country singer Skeeter Davis (real name Mary Penick) enjoyed her biggest ever hit in early 1963 with 'The End Of The World', which was a massive success in both the US pop and country charts, remaining in the country chart for virtually six months; and also became her only UK hit.

Richard Carpenter: "'Da Doo Ron Ron' is one of my favourite Spector/Crystals records and a lot of

fun, and Bob Messenger, one of our group members, who played sax on a lot of our hits, did a really nice solo, and, of course, Tony had the guitar solo in it. The Crystals and the Spector records from this time, and 'Da Doo Ron Ron' in particular, is just so up and so girl group and so much a product of its times that we had to include it. I really like it. And he stopped in - the door opened to Studio B and Phil Spector poked his head in while we were recording this and he said something snide. I can't remember what it was, something like 'Remarkable!' or 'Unbelievable!' then he left."

Also from 1963, 'Da Doo Ron Ron' was the second US Top Three hit in seven months for The Crystals, a female vocal quintet from Brooklyn who were discovered and produced by Phil Spector. It was the earlier of the group's two UK Top Five hits. Richard Carpenter: "Being a Spike Jones fan, I like novelty sound effects, and 'Dead Man's Curve' is just such a bizarre record anyway; I really wanted the crash and the tinkling glass and then of course

I wanted 'Johnny Angel' to come out of that, so 'Dead Man's Curve' was perfect. Plus I like it. I like it a great deal and, and I remember Earl Dumler, who's an oboist, a very talented man we've used for many, many a year, was in when we were sweetening this and two of the tunes that we had in front of him were 'Dead Man's Curve' 'cause he played English horn on that, and 'The End Of The World' and he said 'What is this, a post-mortem medley?' But we had so much fun putting that medley together. If you listen with a keen ear, maybe not even with a keen ear, to the little recitation on 'Dead Man's Curve' you can hear I'm just about ready to lose it: the engineers were in, and Karen, and they were all folded over when I was going 'Well Doc, the last thing I remember I started to swerve', and then I said 'I found out for myself that everyone was right'. I was just about ready to lose it myself."

'Dead Man's Curve' was a 1964 US Top Ten hit for Jan (Berry) & Dean (Torrance), a duo ackowledged as second only to The Beach Boys as pioneers of surf music. Ironically, Jan Berry was so seriously injured in a 1966 car crash which mirrored this song that the duo's career effectively ended at that point.

Richard Carpenter: "'Johnny Angel', which follows 'Dead Man's Curve', was a Number One record in the early Sixties in America. There was a very popular situation comedy called *The Donna Reed Show* with Shelley Fabares and Paul Peterson, and these teen actors were big with the teens, and had recording contracts foisted on them. I heard Shelley talk about this, and she wasn't interested. She said 'I don't know how to sing. I'm not interested in making a record', but she didn't have much choice in the matter. She has a pleasant voice, and it's a beautiful song which was always one of Karen's favourites and it worked perfectly for the vocal harmonies and for Karen to do her girl group 'Sha na sha nas' and that's why that one was included."

Shelley Fabares, who appeared in three Elvis Presley movies, topped the US chart with this song, which was her biggest hit by far, in 1962, when it was also a minor UK hit, peaking outside the Top 40. Richard Carpenter: "I like the chord changes in 'The Night Has A Thousand Eyes', and I liked Bobby Vee's records, the Snuff Garrett productions; Karen and I both did. We listened to both sides of each one like 'Please Don't Ask About Barbara' and 'Be True To Yourself' and, of course, 'Run To Him' and the great Carole King song, 'Take Good Care Of My Baby'; and 'The Night Has A Thousand Eyes' was just one we liked a great deal, which was why we included it."

'Thousand Eyes' was the seventeenth US hit single for Bobby Vee (real name Robert Velline), who was still a teenager when it became his third US Top Three hit in early 1963, and it was also his seventh (and last) UK Top Ten hit. Richard Carpenter: "There was never any question that 'Our Day Will Come' would go in. It's one of my all-time favourite records and songs, and perfect for Karen. It's one of her finest performances. It's low and sensuous and with

Joe Osborn putting in the fluid fills on bass, and it's got that block of background vocals. Obviously, I'm very high on this particular recording."

New York City-born Ruby Nash Curtis fronted Ruby and The Romantics who were based in Akron, Ohio, and whose biggest hit by far was 'Our Day Will Come', which topped the US chart in early 1963 and briefly reached the UK Top 40. Ruby & The Romantics had also recorded an unsuccessful version of 'Hurting Each Other', which The Carpenters had revived on *A Song For You*.

Richard Carpenter: "'One Fine Day' is another one of our favourites, there's just something about it... also it worked in E major, which meant that while it was fading, the reprise of 'Yesterday Once More' could come in." 'One Fine Day' was the US Top Five/UK Top 30 follow-up to 'He's So Fine' for black New York vocal quartet The Chiffons, also in 1963. Richard and Karen had been featuring an oldies medley in their live shows since 1972, but the idea of presenting a string of classics in the form of a radio show (DJ'd by Tony Peluso, complete with phone-in competition and hapless losing contestant, played by associate Mark Rudolph) took the whole idea onto a higher creative level. The Beach Boys classic - with Richard's excellent Mike Love impression! - is an inspired opener, its energy contrasting starkly with the poignant resignation of Karen's delivery of the Skeeter Davis ballad. The contrasts continue, and Karen changes a vocal gear with a spirited rendering of the song generally regarded as one of producer Phil Spector's crowning achievements. A swift pause for the aforementioned phone-in and then it's Richard's second - and equally faithful - rendition of a California cruisin' classic, which fades neatly (if somewhat incongruously) into Karen's take on Shelly Fabares' sugar-sweet chart topper, a splendid example of multi-tracked harmony. Richard rounds off this three song sweep with another energetic near carbon-copy, and with the unlucky phone-in loser disposed of, the final two numbers of the medley showcase Karen's facility with contrasting styles, firstly on the ballad by Ruby And The Romantics before tackling the more upbeat Chiffons classic.

(Two minutes of out-takes from the Radio Contest session were included on the *From The Top* 4xCD set).

YESTERDAY ONCE MORE (REPRISE)
(Carpenter/Bettis)

A sixty second re-recording of the opening line of the original version provides a suitably evocative coda to the medley, seemingly floating out into the ether...

Live In Japan

A&M POCM-1821-2; RELEASED IN 1974, ONLY IN JAPAN.

This double album was apparently released soon after the tour during which it was recorded, and was almost certainly recorded at a time when the popularity of The Carpenters in Japan had reached a periodic crescendo. At time of going to press, this album had not been released anywhere but Japan.

MEDLEY

Superstar (Russell / Bramlett) / Rainy Days And Mondays (Williams / Nichols) / Goodbye To Love (Carpenter / Bettis) / Top Of The World (Carpenter / Bettis) / Help! (Lennon / McCartney)

Some 63 seconds of feedback, tuning up and general audience noise make for a different opening to anyone's album, but once the music starts, there's no mistaking where we are and who we're listening to. Disc One of this 2xCD set opens with a five song medley (which would expand into the ten-strong set of the *Live At The Palladium* album recorded two years later), unusual not only for its inclusion of 'Help' (or per-haps not, considering the enduring pop-ularity of The Beatles in Japan) but also for its extended (and excellent) key-board/guitar workout on the fade. In fact, 'Help' is the highlight of this med-ley, its complex instrumental and vocal tracks being extraordinarily well repro-duced, a tribute to the sterling qualities of The Carpenters' touring band (who are introduced before the next title - see below). The reference to Tony Peluso "catching the plane" apparently refers to a paper plane thrown from the audience.

Musicians: Richard Carpenter (vocals, electric piano, piano, ARP synthesiser), Karen Carpenter (vocals, drums), Cubby O'Brien (drums), Bob Messenger (electric bass, flute, tenor sax), Danny Woodhams (electric bass, vocals), Tony Peluso (guitar, organ, electric bass, ARP synthesiser, narration), Doug Strawn (electric clarinet, organ, vocals), Pete Henderson (vocals).

MR. GUDER
(Carpenter/Bettis)

A concert favourite at this stage of the band's history is presented here with another extended instrumental break, this time featuring Bob Messenger's flute (and briefly the drums), and minus the closing couplet of the studio version. The difficult vocal harmonies are again splendidly performed.

(THEY LONG TO BE) CLOSE TO YOU
(David/Bacharach)

Karen's phrasing may be slightly more 'clipped' in places here than on the original ("just-like-me"), but otherwise the song is just as it always was: a classic, even in a slightly stripped-down live form.

JAMBALAYA (ON THE BAYOU)
(Williams)

How, with just two voices, Richard and Karen manage to almost exactly duplicate multiple studio overdubs, is incredible... but they do, and the result is once more a live version every bit as satisfying as the original.

YESTERDAY ONCE MORE
(Carpenter/Bettis)/
HURTING EACH OTHER
(Udell/Geld)

For this mini-medley, a condensed version (one verse, one chorus) of the first title merges seamlessly into an equally truncated rendition of the second, an indication of just how carefully Richard chose "outside" material sympathetic to his own compositions.

OLDIES MEDLEY

Little Honda (Wilson / Love) / The End Of The World (Dee / Kent) / Runaway (Shannon / Crook) / Da Doo Ron Ron (Barry / Greenwich / Spector) / Leader Of The Pack (Barry / Raleigh) / Johnny Angel (Pockriss / Duddy) / Book Of Love (Davis / Patrick / Malone) / Sh-Boom (Fester / Keyes / McRay / Edward) / Daddy's Home (Sheppard / Miller) / Johnny B. Goode (Berry)

Tony Peluso's DJ intro leads into a medley markedly different to the one which occupied most of side two of *Now And Then*, with only three songs common to both. However, the overall plan remains much the same; replacing 'Fun, Fun, Fun' is another Beach Boys staple from the Sixties by Brian Wilson & Mike Love, which was a US Top Ten hit for The Hondells in 1964 (and a much smaller one for The Beach Boys themselves the same year). Richard handles the lead on a song that may owe its inclusion more to the fact that the band were in Japan than any real fame, or perhaps

motorcycle noises were simpler to arrange than those of a dragster. Del Shannon's 1961 world-wide chart topper features the vocal talents of Pete Henderson (an American comedian/entertainer, who was connected with the opening act, Skyles & Henderson), while the inclusion of The Shangri-Las' 1964 US chart-topper, 'Leader Of The Pack', replaces one death-disc ('Dead man's curve') with another, albeit one well suited to Karen (it's also probably not coincidental that the "leader" is named Johnny...)

Richard returns to centre stage for 'Book Of Love', the 1958 US Top Five for The Monotones (and their only hit), ably supported by Karen on the chorus. All three main vocalists combine excellently for 'Sh-Boom' (spelt on this album as 'Shuboom', for some reason), which is a classic from 1954 recorded by both The Crew-Cuts (a white vocal group who had the bigger hit) and The Chords (a black vocal group who wrote the song and recorded the original version). The 1962 Shep & The Limelites hit, 'Daddy's Home' is handled by Richard, perhaps slightly tongue in cheek; this song was covered by Cliff Richard, whose version all but topped the UK chart over Christmas, 1981. Finally, Pete Henderson and the band get down to some serious rocking with Chuck Berry's eternally classic 1958 US Top Ten hit. All in all, a spirited alternative to the 'official' medley.

SING
(Raposo)

When they were touring, The Carpenters would enlist the help of local schoolchildren to sing backing vocals on this track. Following the introduction of the Kyoto Children's Chorus (entering to the tune of 'Colonel Bogey'!), Karen, and later Richard, make an excellent job of handling a recent hit in the language of the country where they are performing, to the evident delight of the audience.

SOMETIMES
(Mancini/Mancini)

Faithfully recreating the studio version, this showcase for both Richard

and Karen is an ideal vehicle for voice and piano.

WE'VE ONLY JUST BEGUN
(Williams/Nichols)

The live version of the duo's 'signature tune' differs hardly at all from the album recording, even down to the shimmering harmonies.

FOR ALL WE KNOW
(Karlin/Wilson/James)

The title which ends this concert would later (with 'Close To You') be relegated to a place in the 1976 'hits' medley.

Horizon

A&M SP-4530, RELEASED IN JUNE 1975; UK: AMLK 645530; REISSUED AS IN DECEMBER 1990 AS 394530 - 4

Two years after their last original studio album (and following the multi-platinum chart-topping status of *The Singles 1969 - 1973*, which was the only Carpenters album to ever top the Billboard LP chart), *Horizon* emerged at a time when The Carpenters had been an international Premier League act for about five years, with gold albums, loads of hit singles and even Grammy Awards to their credit. However, by this time, musical tastes were changing, and their prolonged absence (probably due to Richard's rumoured quaaludes addiction and a bout of Karen's anorexia), together with new pop stars like The Eagles occupying the airwaves, resulted in a disappointingly brief US chart showing, although *Horizon* followed *The Singles 1969 - 1973* to the top of the UK charts, which was clearly some compensation.

AURORA
(Carpenter/Bettis)

For this small gem of an opening track, John Bettis supplied some of his more enigmatic lyrics to complement Richard's haunting piano figure. Karen, aided by a delicate harp, conveys the mood perfectly.

ONLY YESTERDAY
(Carpenter/Bettis)

For this album, Jim Gordon replaced Karen on drums, and it's his kick drum and snare intro that sets the tone for this rarity amongst Carpenter/Bettis compositions, an initially downbeat song with an ultimately happy ending. Although Bettis admits to its being something of a 'formula' song, it was evidently the right formula as the single release went Top Five in the US and Top Ten in the UK (and cost its composers the $1,000 they bet a studio engineer that it would not be a hit).

John Bettis: "I wouldn't say he's a nostalgia freak rather than being a forward-looking person, but Richard's definitely always been captivated by the past. In his car collection, in his taste in records, and in his ability to remember things. He's absolutely encyclopaedic in his ability to remember songs, and in that regard he is a nostalgic person, much more than I am.

"With 'Only Yesterday', the only pause I had when we sat down to write it was 'Oh boy, here we go again - another yesterday song'. And luckily he put that 'Baby, Baby' section in that song that was sort of Neil Diamond-esque which gave us a different way to go with it, and I found a way to turn it into a positive love song about being in love now, and yesterday was not so good because you weren't here. Perhaps one of the reasons that the friction between us worked is that I'm always throwing songs over my shoulder: next, next, next, next; and Richard, with people, with songs, with everything, when he finds something he likes or something he cherishes, he will keep it forever. That's a positive quality about him, and I think that manifests itself in his nostalgia."

Richard Carpenter: "'Only Yesterday' was a tune that John Bettis and I put together but it was actually meant to sound somewhat like a song from the Sixties, kind of a wall of sound with the castanets and all. It was a combination of Seventies and Sixties, and really, to me, one of our better technical achievements. It's quite a complicated arrangement and took a lot of doing as far as all of the vocals that are on it. It's a difficult song to sing, it's rangy and it starts right off the bat with the low E flat for Karen. It was a difficult mix but Roger Young, who's been with me for many years, engineered it, and it's got lots of little touches in it, little guitar things. It's one of my favourites, actually".

DESPERADO

(Henley/Frey)

A cover version of the title track of the acclaimed 1973 concept album by The Eagles might seem to be a bizarre choice for The Carpenters, but the song's lyrical theme survived to stand up without the album storyline, and also fitted neatly into the style of The Carpenters. Further, Karen's reading picked up on and amplified the inherent melancholy and isolation, a mood highlighted by Tommy Morgan's harmonica.

PLEASE MR. POSTMAN
(Holland/Gorman/Bateman)

Although most people recall the cover version by The Beatles (on their second album, *With The Beatles*), this song was originally a US Number One hit in 1961 for Motown female vocal quintet The Marvelettes. As befits a song from rock's early days, it's simple and undemanding both lyrically and musically (as are many of the most memorable hits from that era), allowing ample room for block harmonies (and featuring Karen's drumming). Sometimes simple is best, as the chart-topping nature of the single version amply demonstrated (the 45 was released some six months before *Horizon*, the album track is a remix).

Richard Carpenter: "For quite a while, I'd felt that 'Please Mr. Postman' could be a very nice record. It was a favourite of ours when The Marvelettes did it, then when The Beatles did it, and we just wanted to do it. And it was done by itself during a

period of time when we were doing a lot of touring and not really recording an album. It's included on *Horizon*, but it was done far before. I wasn't sure whether to release 'Postman' or not: I thought it had commercial potential but I just wasn't sure, for some reason, and that record may have been... I used to think 'Yesterday Once More' was our biggest worldwide, but actually 'Postman' may have been. It was a very big hit in the United States and UK and Germany and Japan and all over. There's just something about 'Please Mr. Postman'. People have mentioned it sounds like we were having such a good time doing it, and we were. It has a lot of joy in it and it's just a simple tune."

I CAN DREAM CAN'T I?
(Kahal/Fain)

A Forties nightclub atmosphere permeates this sumptuous rendering of the old standard, thanks to Billy May's lavish arrangement (with Richard) and orchestration, and the Sisters-style backing vocals.

SOLITAIRE
(Sedaka/Cody)

By the mid-Seventies, Neil Sedaka, a prodigious hitmaker during the somewhat anodyne post-army Elvis/pre-Beatles era of rock, was embarking on a well-received comeback and, while his version (on the album of the same name) wasn't much of a hit, it was a UK Top Five single for Andy Williams in late 1973. Richard knew a good song when he heard it, and developed an arrangement that, as delivered by Karen, truly put the listener through the emotional wringer. Perhaps this was why the single release barely made the US Top 20, the lowest position achieved by The Carpenters since 'Ticket To Ride'. A UK chart placing just outside the Top 30 was equally average.

Richard Carpenter: "I'd heard 'Solitaire' on Neil's 'Solitaire' album and, of course, I heard it by Andy Williams, and, that, to me, is one of the greatest performances of Karen's. It's a very difficult song to sing, she just swallows it whole, she does it so well, and she never liked it. Karen never liked that song, and where she changed her opinion on 'Superstar', she never changed her opinion on 'Solitaire'. She didn't like it, but I still hear it quite a bit in the United States and she sings it so well. It's such a good song for her, and a very melodic, rhapsodic tune."

HAPPY
(Peluso/Rubin/Bettis)

Richard's early experimentation with the ARP Odyssey synthesiser is a feature of this cheerful number that more than lives up to its title. That the production is somewhat sparser than usual is absolutely no handicap at all to a song that might have been a better single choice than the preceding track.

(I'M CAUGHT BETWEEN) GOODBYE AND I LOVE YOU
(Carpenter/Bettis)

Both Richard and Karen were undergoing relationship problems during the recording of *Horizon*, a situation which added a poignant subtext to this lovely ballad of gentle resignation. Again, a restraining hand at the mixing desk adds to the overall sense of melancholy.

LOVE ME FOR WHAT I AM
(Bettis/Pascale)

A companion piece to the preceding track, and in much the same lyrical vein, yet with a harder, more determined edge, is (briefly) brightened by another Tony Peluso fuzz guitar solo. Otherwise, it's a mite too similar to the previous track to be truly effective.

EVENTIDE
(Carpenter/Bettis)

As haunting and mysterious as 'Aurora' as regards lyrics and mood, the track which closes the album features another brief succession of images not usually associated with Carpenters songs.

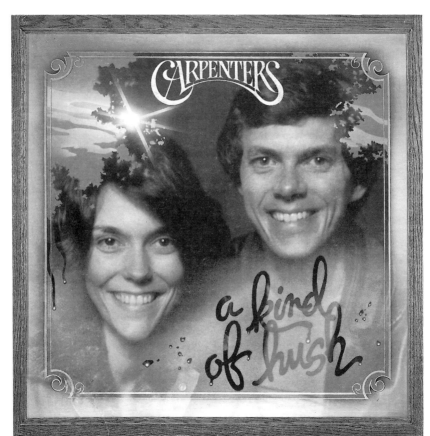

A Kind Of Hush

A&M SP-4581; RELEASED IN MAY 1976; UK: AMLK 64581; REISSUED IN DECEMBER 1990 AS A&M 3931972

This seventh original album is generally felt to be the point where it became clear that a combination of circumstances (their poor health, the changing musical tide, sheer fatigue, etc.) had conspired to prevent The Carpenters maintaining their previously Olympian standards. Of its three excerpted singles, only the title track peaked significantly high (but outside both the US Top Ten and UK Top 20), and the album, despite its gold certification and a high UK chart placing, was a commercial disappointment in the US where its chart peak (outside the Top 30) was a disgrace.

THERE'S A KIND OF HUSH
(Reed/Stephens)

There seemed to be a time during the mid-Sixties when all that was required to score an American chart hit was an English accent and a sufficiently shaggy haircut: how else can you explain the 1967 US Top Five success of the original million-selling version (by Herman's Hermits) of this undeniably slight item (or, some may wonder, that group's 18 US Top 40 hits in under four years)? Richard and Karen's equally lightweight reworking didn't rise to such heights, and although its chart placing was a slight improvement on that of 'Solitaire' it was still cause for some concern.

YOU
(Edelman)

The Carpenters' third cover of a Randy Edelman composition is an album highlight, Richard's arrangement and production admirably supporting one of Karen's more crystalline vocal performances. Once again, Tony Peluso weighs in with a somewhat strident guitar solo.

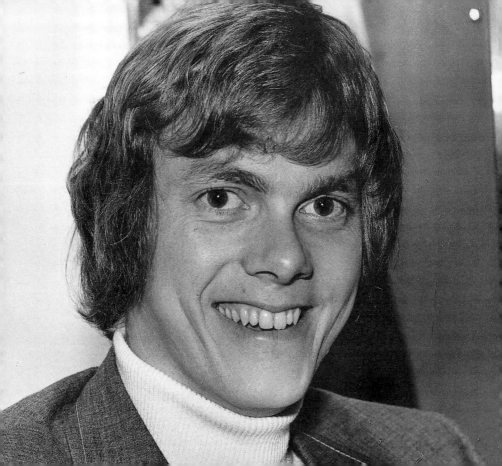

SANDY
(Carpenter/Bettis)

The subject of this song was Karen's assistant/hairdresser, Sandy Holland, whom Richard had once briefly dated (much to his sister's disapproval)... which would explain the slightly bizarre lyrics Karen sings. This aside, it's a sweet little song, albeit of no great weight, featuring excellent harmonies, woodwinds from Tom Scott (a highly celebrated Los Angeles session musician) and even a pair of harp players (as in Harpo Marx).

GOOFUS
(King/Harold/Kahn)

Harking back stylistically to Richard's days at Coke Corner in Disneyland, this pseudo-barbershop number, although ably performed by Karen, was never anything more than album material. Hardly surprising, then, that as a single release (the third from the album), it proved to be the lowest charting Carpenters 45 to date, barely making it

into the mid-fifties in the USA. Wes Jacobs (from the original pre-Spectrum trio) contributes tuba and Bob Messenger the "cheek pop".

CAN'T SMILE WITHOUT YOU
(Arnold/Martin)

A million-selling US Top Three hit in 1978 for Barry Manilow is the version of this song that most people would probably recall, and while this earlier rendition is never less than amiable, it's also pretty unremarkable in all departments.

I NEED TO BE IN LOVE
(Carpenter/Bettis/Hammond)

Easily the best track on the album finds the Carpenter/Bettis team being given assistance from veteran songsmith Albert Hammond. All the elements of the classic Carpenters recipe are here in fine balance, topped by Karen's yearning lead vocal on what was her favourite of all the Carpenters' recordings. As the second single from the album, it was moderately successful in

America (mid-twenties) and less so in the UK (mid-thirties).

John Bettis: "It was very strange. I had been writing songs with Albert. I had met him in England when I was over writing with someone else. We'd met each other at a Joan Armatrading concert, and we were just talking and he said 'We're gonna write together, I'm coming back out to L.A. and we're gonna write together', and I said 'Fine'. So we sat down for a couple of months and tried to write songs but nothing really great happened.

"Albert had a little snippet on a tape, this little orange cassette, and it went 'I Need To Be In Love, I Need To Be In Love', and I kept thinking this is a great title for them. I kept pointing to the title so Albert and I tried to write a song, and we did write something, but it wasn't quite right and I said 'OK, well I gotta show it to Richie anyway', and by the third bar of the chorus, Richard's eyes like lit up and he went 'Yes, I mean yes and no, John, the idea's great and that one little passage is terrific, but it ought to go like this and this and this'. So for

the next afternoon, Richard and I kind of took an existing rough of something that was like a little ball of twine which we unrolled and knitted into a sweater, and by the end it was 'I Need To Be In Love', which is probably the most autobiographical and my favourite lyric I ever wrote for Karen. If there was ever anything that came out of my heart straight to Karen I would say that that was it, and I was very proud of it for that."

ONE MORE TIME
(Anderson)

A neat combination of a stripped-down version of The Carpenters' formula applied to an 'outside' song is a most successful experiment, especially as - unusually - there are absolutely no vocal harmonies to complement Karen's heartfelt rendering of a rather nostalgic lyric.

BOAT TO SAIL
(De Shannon)

Harmonies and sub-Beach Boys vocal stylings abound here, naturally enough given the (vague) subject matter of this item, originally released on Jackie De Shannon's *New Arrangement* album the previous year. A suitably laid back approach pays dividends, and the name check for Brian Wilson (the resident errant genius of The Beach Boys, and creator of the California myth) is a nice touch, even if it did reportedly cause him severe embarrassment. At the end of the track, Karen sings "de Shannon's back", and this has been interpreted as a reference to another A&M act, The Captain & Tennille, singing "Sedaka's back" on their hit version of Neil Sedaka's 'Love Will Keep Us Together'. Was this a slight dig by The Carpenters after they had fallen out with Sedaka? The final track on *A Kind Of Hush* also gives the impression of a certain veiled resentment (see end of chapter).

I HAVE YOU
(Carpenter/Bettis)

Perhaps not the peak achievement of the Carpenter/Bettis partnership, but nonetheless this often overlooked number exerts a strange fascination that's difficult to put a finger on. Again, the restraint of production, performance and arrangement enhances the mood of wry resignation common to so many of the duo's compositions. Karen's expert double-tracking also makes a considerable contribution.

BREAKING UP IS HARD TO DO
(Sedaka/Greenfield)

The absence of any backing vocals from the majority of this curiously lifeless cover of Neil Sedaka's 1962 US chart-topping classic doesn't really do the track any favours. It's competent, but little more, and definitely suffers when compared to the original. See 'Boat To Sail' above for more... In fact, Richard Carpenter arranged the strings on Sedaka's 1975 re-recording of his US Number One, taken at a considerably slower pace than the 1962 original.

DIGITALLY REMASTERED

Live At The Palladium

A&M AMLS - 68403; RELEASED IN 1976; UK: AMLS 64530;

REISSUED IN MARCH 1990 BY PICKWICK RECORDS AS PWKS 572

The reason for the existence of this curiosity is uncertain. The most recent track is 'There's A Kind Of Hush', which was itself only released in 1976, and although this album briefly (three weeks) reached the UK chart, it was probably initially available only for a limited period, although a subsequent CD reissue (on the mid-price Pickwick label) gave it renewed life. However, it remains little more than a curiosity, of more interest to Carpenters completists than to casual buyers, although it is an accurate representation of a live show by The Carpenters. Whatever it was fashionable for rock critics to think about The Carpenters in the first half of the Seventies, my one experience of a live show (at the Royal Festival Hall circa 1972) left me in awe that they were able to reproduce their recorded sound so authentically. It is a matter of great regret to me that there was never a second opportunity for Karen's voice to surround me like a warm blanket, but at least there was a first time, something which the millions of new Carpenters fans will never experience...

FLAT BAROQUE/ ONLY YESTERDAY
(Carpenter; Carpenter/Bettis)

A radical reworking of the track from 1972's *A Song For You* album with a few bars of 'Only Yesterday' thrown in for good measure, makes for a suitably energetic concert intro.

THERE'S A KIND OF HUSH
(Reed/Stephens)

Apart from being taken at a slightly faster clip than the studio version, this is a pretty faithful copy of the album track.

JAMBALAYA
(Williams)

As with the previous track, The Carpenters' ability to almost exactly reproduce the studio version live is evident. Solos by Bob Messenger (flute) and Tony Peluso (guitar) follow name checks for these gents.

PIANO PICKER
(Edelman/Carpenter)

Astute readers will notice a difference in the credits between this and the studio version; that's because Richard (presumably) revised the lyrics to relate more exactly the story of his and Karen's early days (for the uninitiated, Mickey Mantle is a much-revered baseball player: the UK equivalent would be Bobby Charlton).

STRIKE UP THE BAND/S'WONDERFUL/ FASCINATIN' RHYTHM
(Gershwin/Gershwin)

The sole purpose of this brief Gershwin brothers medley is to showcase Karen's drumming talents, to which end it is completely successful.

WARSAW CONCERTO
(Addinsell)

This is Richard's showcase; perhaps a strange choice of material for a pop concert... but then this wasn't a standard pop band. It almost goes without saying that his performance is flawless. However, by all accounts this was not a big hit with fans, and the word "pretentious" has been mentioned in this context.

FROM THIS MOMENT ON
(Porter)

Cole Porter based his classic on Johann Sebastian Bach's 'Prelude No. 2', as is evident from Richard's piano, the sole accompaniment to Karen's excellent vocal. A studio version would remain unreleased until 1994's *Interpretations* compilation CD.

MEDLEY:

(They Long To Be) Close To You (Bacharach / David) / For All We Know (Karlin / Wilson / James) / Top Of The World (Carpenter / Bettis) / Ticket To Ride (Lennon / McCartney) / Only Yesterday (Carpenter / Bettis) / I Won't Last A Day Without You (Williams / Nichols) / Hurting Each Other (Udell / Geld) / Superstar (Russell / Bramlett) / Rainy Days And Mondays (Williams / Nichols) / Goodbye To Love (Carpenter/Bettis)

Quite simply, sixteen and a quarter minutes of 24 carat gold, fourteen minutes of which are music, followed by 45 seconds of applause, after which Richard introduces the band: Danny Woodhams (bass), Cubby O'Brien (drums), Bob Messenger (woodwinds, etc.), Tony Peluso (guitar, etc.) and Doug Strawn (vocals, keyboards, electric clarinet), plus an orchestra. Excepting 'Ticket To Ride', here reduced to a few brief lines, all these titles were US Top Ten hits apart from 'I Won't Last', which peaked one place lower. Each of the songs is presented in a more or less condensed manner, and it says much for the material and the handling of it that this is a medley that doesn't diminish the component parts, and Tony Peluso's solo on 'Goodbye To Love' is every bit as electrifying as on the studio version. One minor query - why wasn't the brilliant (and amusingly well-observed) Spike Jones-styled destruction of 'Close To You' included? Perhaps because it works very effectively visually, but less so without vision as well as sound.

WE'VE ONLY JUST BEGUN
(Williams/Nichols)

What other way to close the album than with The Carpenters' 'signature' tune? As before, a faithful rendition, with the addition of a big band climax and, of course, more rapturous applause.

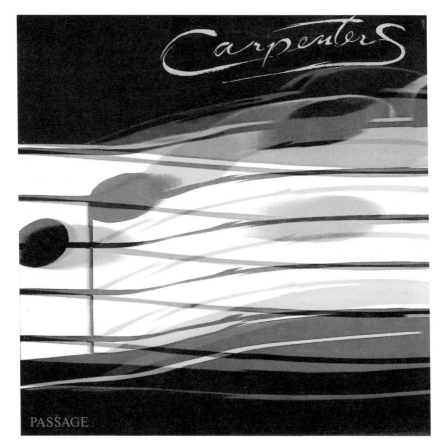

Passage

A&M SP- 4703; RELEASED IN SEPTEMBER 1977; UK : AMLK 64703;
REISSUED IN DECEMBER 1990 AS 393199 - 2

It had been 15 months since *A Kind Of Hush,* which had been a comparative failure by Carpenters standards, peaking outside the Top 30 in the Billboard album chart, and even if they were more popular than ever in the UK (where a mid-price reissue of the début LP, *Ticket To Ride,* had briefly reached the UK Top 30 in the wake of *Horizon* topping the UK chart, and 'Hush' had reached the Top Three), The Carpenters needed to rekindle their massive success in the US, which was the only real gauge they respected. Three US hit singles from an album is hardly the signal to break out the champagne if none of the three gets as high as the Top 30; and as the UK result was two hits, only one of which made the Top Ten, *A Kind Of Hush* could hardly be judged a major commercial success. Apart from the deteriorating state of Karen's health, and Richard's understandable concern for his sister's well-being (not to mention that if they didn't rediscover the appeal which had elevated them to superstardom on this crucial eighth studio album, they might be in permanent decline, if not free fall), this was an important album which had to be made at a highly inappropriate time.

It is a sad fact that the commercial failure of a record leaves an irreversible stain which often inhibits objective criticism thereafter. This really isn't a bad album; The Carpenters were both musically and psychologically incapable of making a genuinely poor album, and the worst accusation that can be made is that for once, Richard failed to judge public taste accurately. Of course, the lack of Carpenter/Bettis material should cause eyebrows to be raised, but in view of Karen's deteriorating condition, probably the last thing Richard felt like doing was writing a happy hit. Everything had to come from outside, and while there are

several obvious hit songs here, perhaps the problems adversely affected the recording sessions. If *Passage* assuredly isn't the best Carpenters album, neither is it the worst, by a long chalk.

B'WANA SHE NO HOME
(Franks)

An intriguing departure from The Carpenters' formula that could be viewed as a daring experiment... or equally as a desperate ploy to turn around a career that was undeniably beginning to show signs of faltering (at least in the USA). At the very least, it's interesting, the production is pin sharp, the salsa-styled track slopes along energetically enough, and Karen's vocals boast an unusually sharp edge. And yet... it somehow fails to convince; to involve the listener.

ALL YOU GET FROM LOVE IS A LOVE SONG
(Eaton)

Despite a mildly tropical backing track, we're pretty much back on familiar ground here, thanks to Richard's arrangement and the lush harmonies. A more successful marriage of classic Carpenters and samba, as the first single released from the album it rose to the mid-thirties in the US charts, a distinct improvement over the previous 45, 'Goofus'. However, due to the peculiar American habit of failing to pronounce the letter 'h' at the start of some words - the rules for this seem obscure, to say the least - this track was featured in a Top Ten of misheard lyrics compiled by British TV & radio celebrity, Noel Edmonds, in the late Seventies. Karen appears to sing "The best loved songs are written with a broken arm"...

I JUST FALL IN LOVE AGAIN
(Dorff/Herbstritt/Skelroy/Lloyd)

The return to home turf is completed by this sweeping ballad, composed of just about every Carpenters' instrumental "trademark" from the opening oboe riff to a Tony Peluso fuzz guitar solo. Vocal harmonies are, however, strangely absent, although not missed. Compared with the two preceding tracks, this has the air of being a leftover or an out-take from a much earlier album, and was considered for release as a single, but rejected due to reasons of length. Ironically, Canadian country star Anne Murray had a US Top 20 hit with her 1979 version.

ON THE BALCONY OF THE CASA ROSADA/DON'T CRY FOR ME ARGENTINA
(Lloyd Webber/Rice)

At 7 minutes 59 seconds, this extract from *Evita* is (medleys excluded) the longest single track in The Carpenters' portfolio, and in that short span of time manages to convey both the best and the worst of Andrew Lloyd Webber's musical spectrum. 'Argentina' is rightly acclaimed as a classic show tune, and Richard was absolutely correct in thinking it a perfect vehicle for Karen (according to Ray Coleman's book on The Carpenters, over objections from Jerry Moss, who considered it a socialist anthem and an overt political statement); her reading is flawless, as is the arrangement. However, the opening 'Casa Rosada' section - featuring an excellent vocal from Dennis Heath as the announcer, and a decidedly dodgy one from William Feuerstein as Juan Peron (Che Guevara's part is sung by Jonathan Marx) - is an example of cod-Opera at its very worst and is, to be frank, ludicrous in both concept (not Richard's fault) and execution (definitely down to him). The orchestration was the work of veteran British music man Peter Knight, who also conducted what the LP sleeve calls the "Overbudget Philharmonic".

SWEET, SWEET SMILE
(Newton/Young)

Perhaps seeking to repeat the unexpected success of 'Top Of The World', Richard turned once again to mildly country-ish domain with this perky item written by country star Juice Newton, replete with banjo and fiddle, and with Ronnie Tutt (from Elvis Presley's band)

on drums. A definite foot-tapper, but not apparently a crowd pleaser, for the single release peaked in the mid-forties in the US and didn't do that much better in the UK. Interestingly, this was the first (and only) country chart hit for The Carpenters, which peaked well into the Top Ten. Incidentally, Juice (Judy Kay) Newton, according to *Billboard*, is "an accomplished equestrian".

Richard Carpenter: "Karen found 'Sweet, Sweet Smile'. A friend of ours is a manager who was representing Juice Newton - this was before she had the number of hits that she went on to have - but, of course, Juice is also a songwriter, and she'd written this piece called 'Sweet, Sweet Smile' that Karen liked, and she said she wanted me to hear it. I liked it immediately: again, it's one of those fun tunes; now there's one that, to me, should have done better than it did. I think had someone else done that tune at that time, it would have been a bigger hit."

TWO SIDES
(Davis)

A more downbeat country number (in lyrical terms, a "quittin'" song) gives a slight hint of where The Carpenters might just have headed had their active career extended beyond 1983. Karen handles a standard country lyric with great aplomb and insight.

MAN SMART, WOMAN SMARTER
(Span)

Reverting to the musical style of the opening track of *Passage*, this eccentric (in both treatment and rhythm) revival of a song from the repertoire of Harry Belafonte gives much support to the theory that this is an album in search of a theme. It is barely Carpenters and, to be honest, barely interesting (even with Leon Russell on piano), with a tedious instrumental fade taking up over half of the song. The song was also recorded during the Seventies by Robert Palmer (backed by four members of Little Feat).

Palmer later wrote in the sleeve note to a compilation CD: "Later on, The Carpenters, of all people, covered this and copied my arrangement to the note. A compliment, I guess, but I still can't understand why." Palmer's CD credits D. Kleiber as the writer of this song.

CALLING OCCUPANTS OF INTERPLANETARY CRAFT (THE RECOGNISED ANTHEM OF WORLD CONTACT DAY)
(Klaatu)

Tony Peluso reprises his excellent DJ act for the intro to this unexpected album highlight, a lengthy (at over seven minutes) opus of changing and contrasting musical styles that became a surprise UK Top Ten hit (and US Top 40 entry). The original version appeared on the eponymous début album of Klaatu, a Canadian five piece whom many people thought might be The Beatles reunited under a pseudonym (nonsense, of course, but such rumours are the lifeblood of rock). Following the release of the single, a large number of people wrote to ask when "World Contact Day" would be! In the notes for *From The Top*, Richard states that there was no such day - incorrectly, according to Andrew Doe, who claims that back in the early Fifties, one of the numerous American 'flying saucer' societies did attempt telepathic contact with anyone "out there", and many of the words of that message are used in this song. The same orchestra and choir (Peter Knight, etc.) are featured on the ending of the song.

Richard Carpenter: "There was an ad campaign in the trades - Who is Klaatu ? Of course, being on Capitol in the United States, [as The Beatles were] the whole thing was supposed to be a reunion of The Beatles. Tony Peluso, who calls himself 'a Beatle Baby', was going on and on about this album and I'd seen the ad., but I hadn't been to the record store in a while. So he said 'You have to hear it, you've got to hear...' he mentioned 'Subrosa Subway' and 'Calling Occupants Of Interplanetary Craft', and right off the bat, being a sci-ence fiction fan, I had to listen to this. I knew immediately it wasn't The Beatles, but it was very well done, very, very Beatlesque. And the more I listened to it, just out of entertainment, I started thinking this would be a lot of fun to do with Karen. Where Klaatu used mostly synthesizers, I thought it was such a production we ought to get a symphony and a choir and a pipe organ and we can have Tony do one of his patented, as Tom Nolan called it, *Apollonian* guitar solos. We could have a ball with this piece, and that's how it came to be."

CARPENTERS

Christmas Collection

Christmas Portrait

A&M SP- 4762; RELEASED IN OCTOBER 1978; UK:

REISSUED IN 1990 AS A&M 3851732

Richard & Karen Carpenter seemingly never lost the youthful enthusiasm for Christmas which, unfortunately, disappears for many during adolescence, and by all accounts, they greatly enjoyed this project, so much so that they recorded far too much material simply because they were having such a good time. After Karen's death, Richard was able to assemble a second festive album, An Old-Fashioned Christmas, which was released in 1985.

O Come, O Come Emmanuel (Public Domain, arranged & adapted Richard Carpenter)/Overture: Deck The Halls (Public Domain, Traditional French Carol/I Saw Three Ships (Public Domain, Traditional Welsh Carol/Overton)/Have Yourself A Merry Little Christmas (Hugh Martin/Ralph Blane)/God Rest Ye Merry Gentlemen (Public Domain, Traditional English Carol)/Away In A Manger (Luther's Cradle Hymn) (Public Domain, Anon., Murray)/What Child Is This? (Greensleeves) (Public Domain, Will C.Dix)/Carol Of The Bells (Public Domain, Traditional Ukrainian Carol, arranged & adapted by Nick Perito, Peter Knight)/

O Come All Ye Faithful (Adeste Fideles) (Public Domain, Fred Oakeley, John Wade)/The Christmas Waltz (Sammy Cahn/Jule Styne)/Sleigh Ride (Mitchell Parish/Leroy Anderson)/It's Christmas Time (Victor Young/Al Stillman); Sleep Well, Little Children (Alan Bergman/Leon Klatzkin)/Have Yourself A Merry Little Christmas (Hugh Martin/Ralph Blane)/Santa Claus Is Coming To Town (Haven Gillespie/Fred Coots)/The Christmas Song (Chestnuts Roasting On An Open Fire) (Mel Torme/Robert Wells)/Silent Night (Public Domain, originally by Franz Gruber, arranged & adapted Peter Knight)/Jingle Bells (Public Domain, originally by James Pierpont, arranged &

adapted Peter Knight)/The First Snowfall (Joseph F.Burke/Paul Francis Webster); Let It Snow, Let It Snow, Let It Snow (Sammy Cahn/Jule Styne)/Carol of The Bells (Traditional Ukrainian Carol, arranged & adapted Nick Perito/Peter Knight)/Merry Christmas, Darling (Frank Pooler/Richard Carpenter)/I'll Be Home For Christmas (Kim Gannon/Buck Ram/Walter Kent)/Christ Is Born (Ray Charles/Dominico Bartolucci)/Winter Wonderland (Dick Smith/Felix Bernard); Silver Bells (Jay Livingston/Ray Evans); White Christmas (Irving Berlin)/Ave Maria (Public Domain, originally by Johann Sebastian Bach/Charles Gounod, arranged & adapted Peter Knight)

Introduced by an atmospheric multi-tracked a cappella rendering by Richard, an instrumental overture sets the scene, and tone, for a classic of the Christmas genre, and also a perfect showcase for Karen's solo vocals, augmented on most songs by the Tom Bahler Chorale (who have their own featured vocal on 'Silver Bells'). The arrangement for most of the

vocal titles ('Carol Of The Bells' is a further instrumental interlude) is in a vaguely Forties movie style, the major exceptions being gloriously evocative performances of 'Silent Night' and 'Ave Maria' (the latter also appears on *From The Top* augmented by a full choir); and the 1970 seasonal Carpenters single, 'Merry Christmas Darling', presented here with a newly recorded lead vocal (*From The Top* includes the original version). Richard and Karen had actually been performing 'Merry Christmas Darling' since 1966, when Richard's choirmaster at college, Frank Pooler, asked him to set a 20-year-old lyric to music. The whole album is, quite simply, a perfect expression of the Christmas spirit. Note some interesting names among the composer credits: Sammy Cahn & Jule Styne, Victor Young, Mel Torme, Buck Ram, Ray Charles, and Irving Berlin (of course). While this is hardly competition for the Phil Spector Christmas album (widely regarded as the best and most imaginative of modern times), it is still a delightful collection.

Made In America

A&M SP-4954; RELEASED IN JUNE 1981; UK: AMLK 63723;
REISSUED IN 1990 ON CD IN THE UK AS 393723 -2

This was the first new (non-festive) Carpenters album for three and a half years and the last complete album on which Karen Carpenter participated. While it cannot be claimed that this is the equal of the great Carpenters LPs, it is probably better than *Passage*, and not inferior to *A Kind Of Hush*. Its failure to reach the Top 50 of the US chart is hardly surprising: nothing new for far too long (bar the Christmas album); the fickle nature of record buyers; the lack of a Top Ten single; a disappointing last LP and, perhaps most significantly, a general perception that The Carpenters were past their "sell by" date. In terms of new recordings, the last item in that list was true, but the unimaginable success of their back catalogue in the Nineties makes it clear that this music is timeless, and has very little to do with fads and fashions. Britain remembered, and although there were no UK hit singles on the album (as opposed to four hit singles, three of them very minor, in the US), the LP upheld their proud record of making the UK Top 20 with every regular studio album. A reasonable farewell from an extraordinary performer with a voice of incredible quality...

Surprisingly, this is, generally speaking, the favourite of Carpenters fans, especially young fans, which may be explained by the fact that it has a more modern feel than earlier albums, which more mature fans regard as far superior.

THOSE GOOD OLD DREAMS
(Carpenter/Bettis)

The Carpenter/Bettis magic, so badly missed on *Passage*, makes a most welcome return on this cheerful, mildly country-flavoured song that sports a lyric made significant by later, tragic, events. Karen's vocal is more than usually mellow while Richard's production exhibits a new clarity and precision. As the third single culled from the album, it truly deserved better than a US chart placing outside the Top 50.

STRENGTH OF A WOMAN
(Brown/Curiel)

The juxtaposition of a reflective verse with an assertive chorus elevates this track from mere album material to something rather special, as does Karen's conversational reading of a lyric that, in less sure hands, could have degenerated into a country cliché. The change of gear in the middle-eight catches the ear at just the right moment, and the use of other backing vocalists adds just the right degree of stridency to the chorus.

(WANT YOU) BACK IN MY LIFE AGAIN
(Chater/Christian)

Pitched just the acceptable side of disco, this light electro-pop number provided a telling contrast with the album's two opening tracks, and again it's the chorus - with a very upfront kick drum riff providing a neat hook - that catches the listener's interest. Karen's verse vocals,

by comparison, sound slightly formulaic: competent but hardly involved or involving. Perhaps that's why, as the second 45 taken from the LP, this song briefly held the unwanted distinction of being The Carpenters' lowest ever US charting single, just reaching the US Top 75. Two names are credited with "synthesizer programming" (sic), Daryl Dragon (aka The Captain of Captain & Tennille and a member of The Beach Boys in the early Seventies) and Ian Underwood (presumably the erstwhile longtime member of Frank Zappa's Mothers Of Invention).

WHEN YOU'VE GOT WHAT IT TAKES
(Nichols/Lane)

Never less than pleasant, this mid-tempo number (recalling 'I Kept On Loving You' from *Close To You*) is still somehow possessed of a sense of vagueness, even though both the performance and production are well up to standard. The horn riffs during the chorus are, however, a neat touch.

SOMEBODY'S BEEN LYIN'
(Bayer Sager/Bacharach)

A sumptuous Bacharach melody, replete with the unusual lyrical phrasing for which he was noted ('Do You Know The Way To San Jose ?' is the prime example) is expertly, almost effortlessly, handled by Karen; while the air of resigned realisation outlined in Carol Bayer Sager (a Mrs.Bacharach)'s lyric is underscored by Richard's nicely restrained arrangement.

I BELIEVE YOU
(Addrisi/Addrisi)

Originally released as the first single from the album in late 1978, this cover of Dorothy Moore's 1977 Top 30 hit stands slightly apart from the rest of the album due to a minor yet obvious difference in the overall production values: it's that touch lusher. This aside, it's an acceptable album cut, but not really 45 material, as a US chart placing in the low sixties (The Carpenters' lowest ranking at that date) would seem to confirm.

TOUCH ME WHEN WE'RE DANCING
(Skinner/Wallace/Bell)

When all the ingredients gelled, the result was irresistible... and that's just what we have here, a perfect Carpenters confection, reminiscent of the classic days of the early Seventies. For one last time, the record buying public agreed, making this second single to be pulled from *Made In America* the final US Top 20 hit of Richard and Karen's career.

WHEN IT'S GONE (IT'S JUST GONE)
(Handley)

Once again, Karen's sensitive reading rescues this country-style item from descending into a series of clichés. The predominantly acoustic instrumental track pushes the song along very nicely indeed.

BEECHWOOD 4-5789
(Stevenson/Gaye/Gordy)

Richard's intriguingly percussive arrangement of the 1962 US Top 20 hit by Motown girl group The Marvelettes (of 'Please Mr. Postman' fame), which is one of the great telephone number songs (like Wilson Pickett's '634-5789') certainly catches the ear, and the massed vocals are spot on; but evidently something failed to click, and this fourth single to be taken from the album became not only The Carpenters' lowest charting US 45 (just below '(Want You) Back In My Life Again') but also their final US singles chart entry ever.

BECAUSE WE ARE IN LOVE (THE WEDDING SONG)
(Carpenter/Bettis)

Written expressly for, and first performed at Karen's 1980 wedding to Tom Burris, Richard's ambition of having this sound "like a show tune" was splendidly realised with able assistance from English arranger Peter Knight (who had previously worked with The Moody Blues). An impressionistic, almost tentative introduction gives way to a suitably opulent composition expressing all the emotions of the impending bride, impeccably backed by the choir during the middle eight. Sadly, the marriage lasted less than two years - and Karen died less than two years after *Made In America* was released.

CARPENTERS

VOICE OF THE HEART

Voice Of The Heart

A&M SP - 4954; RELEASED IN OCOBER 1983 ; UK : AMLX64954;

REISSUED IN 1988 AS CDA 4954

After Karen's death on February 4, 1983 of "heart failure due to anorexia nervosa" (according to *Billboard*), Richard assembled this album, which once again peaked outside the Top 40 of the US album chart (although it interestingly spent more weeks on that chart than any original Carpenters album since Now And Then, had done ten years before); and in the UK, peaked higher than either *Passage* or *Made In America,* and spent considerably longer in the chart than either, perhaps because it included a hit single, albeit a minor one, but still their first for five and a half years.

NOW
(Nichols/Pitchford)

If it sounds slightly as if Karen isn't perhaps putting her all into the vocal of this lovely ballad... well, in truth she wasn't, but only because she was laying down a work vocal during the instrumental track session, a recording which would normally later be wiped and replaced with a properly rehearsed and phrased lead. That said, it's still a wonderfully emotive rendition, pitched slightly higher than usual. This was recorded during Karen's last-ever session, and as with most of the songs on *Voice Of The Heart*, was finished up and fine tuned by Richard after her untimely death: this may account for a slight sense of detachment concerning the backing vocals. They're splendid - but they're not The Carpenters. Richard has been quoted as saying that Karen had never sounded better, although some fans apparently feel that her voice sounds weak.

SAILING ON THE TIDE
(Peluso/Bettis)

Contrasting starkly with the preceding track in both mood and topic, this perky little calypso-ish number is helped to rest more easily on the ear by the presence of Karen on the backing vocals. It is a song of no great merit, but is in no way objectionable at all, just a pleasant way of passing a few minutes.

YOU'RE ENOUGH
(Carpenter/Bettis)

With a piano introduction strongly reminiscent of 'You' from *A Kind Of Hush*, this composition from the long standing partnership harks back equally strongly to the golden era of the mid-Seventies (a sense heightened by a neat horn riff during the fade) even though its lyric is generally upbeat.

MAKE BELIEVE IT'S YOUR FIRST TIME
(Morrison/Wilson)

Karen recorded the original version of this touchingly tentative appeal to a new lover during the New York sessions for her aborted solo album, and it's interesting that Richard (who had a generally low opinion of the project) eventually felt this song worthy of inclusion on a Carpenters album. As might be expected, this is a somewhat lusher rendering, with the addition of backing vocals and, were it not for the lack of a Phil Ramone co-production credit and the inclusion of a previously non-existent middle eight, it would be all too easy to assume that the lead vocal track is the original recording: Karen's recreation is note perfect. The only single released from the album, it just cracked the UK Top 60 but failed to chart in the US.

TWO LIVES
(Jordan)

A questioning country style lyric sits comfortably on a largely acoustic instrumental backing track, and benefits immensely from both a sensitive reading from Karen (amazingly, this is apparently a work lead), and a light production from Richard. Songwriter Mark Jordan is a musician who has appeared on albums by the likes of Van Morrison and Dave Mason, and among those playing on this track are guitarist Fred Tackett (later of Little Feat), drummer Larrie Londin (who worked for many years with The Everly Brothers) and celebrated pedal steel player Jay Dee Maness. This was an outtake from the *Made In America* sessions, and Richard first heard this song on Bonnie Raitt's first gold album, 1977's *Sweet Forgiveness.*

AT THE END OF A SONG
(Carpenter/Bettis)

Marimba, accordion and guitar impart a distinctly Mexican flavour to this mildly downbeat number, bouyed up by an excellent vocal from Karen and a neat melodic twist on the chorus.

ORDINARY FOOL
(Williams)

This song was originally recorded some seven years earlier, during the session for the *A Kind Of Hush* album, a fact which explains the somewhat warmer production ambience (a feature which should have been at odds with the mournful lyric and vocal, but somehow wasn't). It's a splendid 'late night/cocktail lounge' type of number, undeserving of such a belated release.

PRIME TIME LOVE
(Unobsky/Ironstone)

A fractured yet strangely compelling arrangement catches the ear more than any other aspect of this example of a perfect album filler. The instrumental track is crisp, the vocals incisive and yet there's an air of aimlessness here.

YOUR BABY DOESN'T LOVE YOU ANYMORE
(Weiss)

A faintly ominous bass intro soon gives way to what could be unkindly described as "formula Carpenters"... but thankfully, that formula included Karen's sublime voice, here counter-pointed by some classic brother/sister backing vocals. This might have been a better choice of single.

LOOK TO YOUR DREAMS
(Carpenter/Bettis)

This 1978 recording was relegated to the A&M tape archives largely due to Richard's feeling that it didn't have a contemporary feel (since when did that bother them?). As with 'Ordinary Fool', the production ambience hints at this ballad's true age, but it still sits neatly enough with the overall album mood, although the backing vocals may well have been revised or added in 1983. The song was originally written, at Karen's request, way back in 1974. This was apparently Agnes Carpenter's favourite.

An Old-Fashioned Christmas

A&M SP-3270; RELEASED IN OCTOBER 1984; UK: AMA 3270;

Richard & Karen had approached the *Christmas Portrait* project with such enthusiasm that a large number of unused (and in some cases unfinished) tracks remained unreleased. Such was the continuing demand for Carpenters Christmas product that in 1984 Richard decided to combine the unused tracks with some new recordings (including a new Carpenter/Bettis composition in the title song, and the B-side of the 1970 Christmas 45, 'Santa Claus Is Coming To Town') to produce a second volume of seasonal songs. Much of the additional recording was undertaken at London's Abbey Road studios, renowned as the home of The Beatles. Karen's vocal appearance is held off until the fifth track, and as before she shares the vocal chores, this time with The O.K. Chorale. Again, Richard sets the scene with an a cappella intro. Unavoidably, there are more choral vocals and instrumental selections this time, but even so it's Karen's voice that shines, most notably on a shimmering 'Little Altar Boy' and a poignant duet with her brother on 'Do You Hear What I Hear?'. The inclusion of 'My Favourite Things' from the movie The Sound Of Music may raise the odd eyebrow, but even so, this is a worthy companion piece to *Christmas Portrait*. Other noteworthy writers of material here include famous silver screen cowboy Gene Autry, Frank Loesser (who also wrote the songs for the celebrated musical, 'Guys & Dolls') and the poet Henry Wadsworth Longfellow.

In 1989, for the release of the 12xCD set of The Carpenters' entire catalogue (barring compilations and the UK only live album), the best of both Christmas albums were combined to form a single seventy-minute CD. However, demand was such that in 1996 A&M released a double CD entitled *Christmas Collection*, comprising both original albums.

It Came Upon A Midnight Clear (Sears/Willis) Overture: Happy Holiday (Irving Berlin)/The First Noel (Public Domain - Old English Carol)/March Of The Toys (Victor Herbert)/Little Jesus (Public Domain - from the Oxford Book Of Carols)/I Saw Mommy Kissing Santa Claus (Tommie Connor)/O Little Town Of Bethlehem (Public Domain - L.H.Redner)/In Dulce Jubilo (Public Domain - 14th Century German melody)/Gesu Bambino (The Infant Jesus) (Pietro A. Yon)/Angels We Have Heard On High (Public Domain - Traditional French Carol)An Old-Fashioned Christmas (Carpenter/Bettis) O Holy Night (Public Domain - Adolphe Adam/adapted by Richard Carpenter) (There's No Place Like) Home For The Holidays (Allen/Stillman) Medley: Here Comes Santa Claus Autry/Haldeman)/Frosty the Snowman (Nelson/Rollins) /Rudolph The Red-Nosed Reindeer (Marks)/Good King Wenceslas (Public Domain - John Mason Neale/adapted by Richard Carpenter)/Little Altar Boy

(Smith)/Do You Hear What I Hear? (Regney/Shane)/My Favourite Things (Rodgers/Hammerstein)/He Came Here For Me (Nelson)/Santa Claus Is Comin' To Town (Gillespie)/What Are You Doing New Year's Eve? (Loesser)/Selections From 'The Nutcracker': a: Overture Miniature b: Dance Of The Sugar Plum Fairy c: Trepak d: Valse Des Fleurs (Public Domain - Peter Tchaikovsky/adapted by Richard Carpenter) I Heard The Bells On Christmas Day (Marks/Longfellow)

From The Top

A&M 7 31454 0000 - 2; RELEASED SEPTEMBER 1991

Following the success of the limited edition 12 CD boxed set, The Compact Disc Collection (see the 'Compilations' chapter below), Richard Carpenter assembled this 4 CD unlimited edition boxed set

Full track listing (# denotes a previously unreleased song or new version, *indicates additional recording and/or a remix) is as folows:

CD 1 (1965-1970):

Caravan# / The Parting Of Our Ways# / Looking For Love# / I'll Be Yours# / Iced Tea# / You'll Love Me# / All I Can Do# / Don't Be Afraid# / Invocation# / Your Wonderful Parade# / Goodnight# / All Of My Life* / Eve* / Ticket To Ride (1973 version) / Get Together# / Interview# / Maybe It's You* / (They Long To Be) Close To You* / We've Only Just Begun* / Merry Christmas, Darling (single version) / For All We Know*

CARAVAN
(Mills/Ellington)

Performed by The Richard Carpenter Trio - the third member being Wes Jacobs on stand-up bass - this 1965 home recording of the Duke Ellington standard was arranged by Richard with the express aim of affording each musician a solo spot. As can be heard from the odd sneezes and giggles, this was a live recording, without the benefit of overdubs. As can also be heard, 18-year-old Richard and 15-year-old Karen were astonishingly proficient on their chosen instruments.

THE PARTING OF OUR WAYS

(Carpenter)

Recorded in 1966 in Joe Osborn's garage studio, this unimpressive performance of an average song in no way hints at the glories to come, but is nonetheless of historical interest. The poor sound quality is due to the song being a copy of a well-used acetate disc, the original tapes having been lost in a 1975 fire at Osborn's house.

LOOKING FOR LOVE

(Carpenter)

Osborn was also part owner of Magic Lamp Records, who signed Karen in mid-1966, and this unremarkable item is the A-side of her first (and only) solo single, of which only 500 were pressed. This track is taken from one of those singles, hence the poor quality of the sound.

I'LL BE YOURS

(Carpenter)

The B-side of Karen's solo single is pretty much more of the same, although her vocal ability seems to be expanding.

ICED TEA

(Carpenter)

With this bizarre composition, a jazz-styled waltz featuring a tuba (played by Wes Jacobs), The Richard Carpenter Trio won the annual Los Angeles 'Battle Of The Bands' in 1966, a success which led to them being signed (briefly) to RCA Records. After cutting eleven songs in rapid time, the company decided not to take up its option, and lost a fortune (although it is only fair to note that any label which failed to recognise star quality could suffer a similar fate, for example, Decca Records turning down The Beatles).

YOU'LL LOVE ME
(Carpenter)

After Jacobs left The Trio, Richard and Karen teamed up with three of Richard's fellow choir members at the California State University at Long Beach (including one John Bettis) to form Summerchimes. Their then manager obtained time at a local studio and this is one of nine titles cut during a single long session. Reminiscent of both The Byrds and The Beatles, it was something of a blind alley for Richard: pleasant but not representative. Other than Richard (electric piano, vocals), Karen (lead vocals, drums) and John Bettis (guitar, vocals), the other members of this quintet were Gary Sims (guitar, vocals) and Danny Woodhams (bass, vocals) - Sims and Woodhams later became members of the road group backing The Carpenters.

ALL I CAN DO
(Carpenter, Bettis)

This song later appeared on *Offering*, but this earlier version was by Spectrum, the sextet which grew out of Summerchimes. The additional member was a second female vocalist, Leslie Johnston. This song was originally recorded in the Carpenter home, with echo effects achieved by recording in the tiled bathroom; but on this version, echo was added in the studio.

GOODNIGHT
(Lennon/McCartney)

Richard provided this restful arrangement of the track from *The Beatles* for the California State University, Long Beach (CSULB) choir, here backing Karen in 1969, some months before the release of the début album by The Carpenters. Her vocal range and delivery are much improved, even when heard through the pops and clicks of the vinyl LP from which this track was taped.

INTERVIEW

Definitely to be filed under "historical interest only", this extremely stilted interview follows on from a live rendition of 'Get Together' recorded for the Public Service Programme, *Your Navy Presents*. As Richard points out in the *From The Top* notes, "interesting if for no other reason than to listen to the vernacular of the day". Did anybody ever really talk like that?

CD 2 (1971-1973):

Superstar* / Rainy Days And Mondays* / Let Me Be The One* / Bless The Beasts And Children* / Hurting Each Other* / Top Of The World (original LP version) / Goodbye To Love* / Santa Claus Is Coming To Town* / This Masquerade* / Canta-Sing# (Spanish lyric) / Yesterday Once More* / Medley: Fun, Fun, Fun, The End Of The World, Da Doo Ron Ron, Deadman's Curve, Johnny Angel, The Night Has A Thousand Eyes, Our Day Will Come, One Fine Day* / Yesterday Once More (reprise) / Radio Contest Outtakes#

RADIO CONTEST OUTTAKES

An instructive and amusing insight into just how easy it is to work efficiently in the recording studio. From her comments, Karen is evidently supplying the drum rolls, and a fine time is being had by all... except Tony Peluso.

CD 3 (1974-1978):

Please Mr. Postman / Only Yesterday / Solitaire / Good Friends Are For Keeps#* / Ordinary Fool / I Need To Be In Love* / From This Moment On (live) / Suntory Pop Jingles#*/All You Get From Love Is A Love Song / Calling Occupants Of Interplanetary Craft* / Christ Is Born* / White Christmas* / Little Altar Boy / Ave Maria#*

GOOD FRIENDS ARE FOR KEEPS

(Silberman)

This songlet, recorded in a generally good-time style, was part of a Ma Bell (Bell Telephone Company) advertising campaign.

SUNTORY POP JINGLES
(Suzuki/Narahashi-Umegaki-Narahashi)

Given that The Carpenters were (and are) hugely popular in Japan, it seemed natural for them to do some promotion work in that country. However, the lyrics for these adverts for a soft drink may have lost something in the translation.

CD 4 (1978-1982):
If I Had You* / My Body Keeps Changing My Mind#* / Still Crazy After All These Years#* / Medley # / Touch Me When We're Dancing / When It's Gone / Because We Are In Love / No

Medley: Sing (Raposo) / Knowing When To Leave (Bacharach / David) / Make It Easy On Yourself (Bacharach / David) / Someday (Carpenter / Bettis) / We've Only Just Begun (Nichols / Williams)

As the final item for their 1980 ABC-TV Special, Richard concocted this medley of some of the earliest songs he and Karen had recorded. A 40-second frag-ment of 'Sing' gives way to the first of two Bacharach/David compositions, each performed pretty much in full (and not unlike the Bacharach/David medley on the *Carpenters* album). There follows a two-minute version of 'Someday' (from *Offering*, which enabled Karen to re-record a vocal with which she had apparently never been particularly happy) before a condensed yet lush version of The Carpenters' 'theme song' completes the medley. Splendid.

Lovelines

A&M CD-3931; RELEASED OCTOBER 1989; UK: AMA 3931; REISSUED IN 1990 CDA 3931

Although there had been no new Carpenters album for six years (apart from the second Christmas album), there was still considerable interest in their music, fuelled to some extent by the release of a "made for TV" bio-pic, *The Karen Carpenter Story*, starring Cynthia Gibb in the title role, which apparently topped the ratings in the US at the start of 1979. When this was screened in the UK, it triggered the re-entry into the UK chart of the two compilations (*The Singles 1969-1973* and *The Singles 1974-1978*), and also gave *Lovelines* its sole week in the UK chart.

LOVELINES
(Temperton)

Originally recorded for Karen's then-unreleased solo album (see *Karen Carpenter*), this track is presented here in a remixed (by Richard, one assumes) version that is also about thirty seconds shorter than previously. The most obvious difference is in the placement of the backing vocals: overall, this version boasts a softer, less strident feel.

WHERE DO I GO FROM HERE ?
(McGee)

In 1978, between the releases of the *Passage* and *Christmas Portrait* albums, Richard and Karen recorded a number of songs which, apart from the 'I Believe You' single, remained unreleased for several years - unjustly so, in the case of this aching and questioning ballad of a love turned cold. Karen's lead is totally unadorned by any harmonies, to great effect... and there's a trademark Tony Peluso fuzz guitar solo, too.

THE UNINVITED GUEST
(Kaye/Tweel)

Recorded during the 1980 *Made In America* sessions. The theme of this song - that of there being "another woman" - effortlessly includes every possible cliché that the subject affords, and could have been simply another country stereotype. Yet in Karen's hands (ably supported by Richard's gentle and spare production) it assumes an air of resigned poignancy that is most affecting.

IF WE TRY
(Temperton)

Another track from Karen's solo album, this remix is less obvious than that of 'Lovelines'.

WHEN I FALL IN LOVE
(Heyman/Young)

Best known from Nat 'King' Cole's eternally classic 1957 version, the melody was originally featured in a 1951 film, *One Minute To Zero*. This Forties-style arrangement (by Peter Knight) was recorded - with 'Little Girl Blue' - for the 1978 Carpenters ABC TV special, *Space Encounters*, but lost out to the latter title and was eventually included in another ABC TV Special, *Music, Music, Music*, in 1980.

KISS ME THE WAY YOU DID LAST NIGHT
(Lawley/Dorn)

Another *Made In America* outtake. The splendid chorus harmonies and backing vocals go a long way to redeeming this meandering song that never really seems to get going in any particular direction. The story goes that this item was not released previously because it was extremely difficult to mix down to a stereo version, but technological advances finally made it possible.

REMEMBER WHEN LOVIN' TOOK ALL NIGHT
(Farrar/Leiken)

The third extract from Karen's solo project is once again the recipient of a barely detectable remix.

YOU'RE THE ONE
(Ferguson)

A *Passage* outtake from 1977, this lush ballad was excluded from that album as being too similar to 'I Just Fall In Love Again', which is a shame, as it's distinctly preferable to several of the tracks on that album.

HONOLULU CITY LIGHTS
(Beamer)

Another of the 1978 recordings. The title and part of the lyric are somewhat at odds with the semi-country treatment and, in truth, Karen's effortless lead vocal is pretty much the only point of interest in this run of the mill composition. While it had never previously appeared on either a US or UK release, the song had been included on *Anthology*, a 1989 Japanese double CD (see compilations section below).

SLOW DANCE
(Margo)

Also recorded in 1978, this lazily good-humoured number would have fitted easily on Karen's solo album

IF I HAD YOU
(Dorff/Harju/Herbstritt)

The final track here extracted from the *Karen Carpenter* album undergoes about as extensive a revision as 'Lovelines' and although, once again, the backing vocals are the most evidently reworked, this time there are minor yet discernible differences in the instrumental track.

LITTLE GIRL BLUE
(Rodgers/Hart)

Featured in The Carpenters' 1978 ABC TV special, this Thirties standard (arranged by Peter Knight) forms an excellent companion piece to 'When I Fall In Love'.

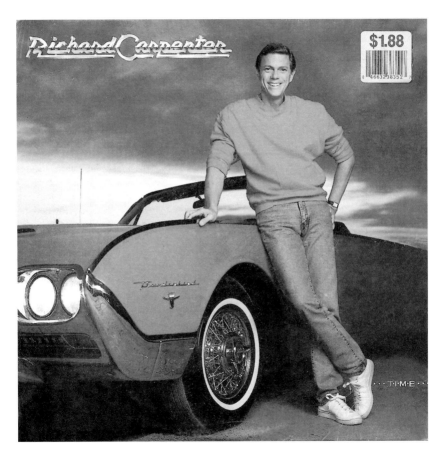

Richard Carpenter Time

(RELEASED OCTOBER, 1987)

This solo album was an interesting attempt by Richard to use some established talents (and one unknown) to sing some of the songs he had written with several collaborators (including, of course, John Bettis). It cannot have been easy to find any female vocalist who would willingly and inevitably submit to comparison with Karen, but both Dusty Springfield and Dionne Warwick were sufficiently famous with recognisable vocal styles (and pre-dated the era when The Carpenters were most influential), while 15 year old Scott Grimes was a) male and b) largely unknown. Many of the musicians are familiar names: Joe Osborn, Tony Peluso, even Herb Alpert, and this is a creditable album which was only briefly available on CD and has been long deleted - although it will undoubtedly re-emerge eventually.

SAY YEAH !
(Janz/Phillips Oland)

Richard's decision to kick the album off with the startlingly contemporary sound of this spirited number may have come as something of a shock to fans of the 'old-style', but it's undeniably an energetic song, and one eminently suited to multiple vocal overdubs. Perhaps the chorus might have been stronger, but otherwise, impressive. Lead vocal: Richard Carpenter.

WHO DO YOU LOVE ?
(Holden/Hamilton/Pickus)

A simple pop song, nothing more nor less, but executed with great panache and good humour: Richard's longtime love of The Beach Boys is evident in the vocal arrangement and verse backing vocals. Lead vocal: Richard Carpenter.

SOMETHING IN YOUR EYES
(Carpenter/Phillips Oland)

Splendid though Dusty Springfield's lead vocal is (and this is no exaggeration), one can't help thinking how this ballad, styled in the classic Carpenters mould, might have sounded with a vocal from Karen. Probably not too dissimilar, but her intangible touch of magic might have made a great song superb.

WHEN TIME WAS ALL WE HAD (A DEDICATION TO KAREN)
(Carpenter/Phillips Oland)

The influence of Brian Wilson and The Beach Boys is even more evident during Richard's multi-tracked a cappella opening section of this heartfelt tribute to his sister. Herb Alpert supplies what Richard calls "the moving flugelhorn solo" during the instrumental portion. It has been observed by certain Carpenters fans that it seems surprising that John Bettis was not Richard's collaborator in writing this song...

TIME
(Carpenter)

An amiable enough, yet meandering, instrumental is highlighted by Richard's imaginative use of the synthesizer.

CALLING YOUR NAME AGAIN
(Carpenter/Marx)

Something of a power ballad before the term was coined, this is an excellent number with well-above average lyrics from contemporary pop star Richard Marx and a gently understated lead vocal from Richard.

IN LOVE AGAIN
(Carpenter/Bettis)

Dionne Warwick provides a trademark silky lead vocal to the thought, again, of "what if?" on this welcome reunion of the old songwriting partnership. Such comparisons are unfair but inescapable.

REMIND ME TO TELL YOU
(Mueller)

A faintly ominous verse, a superb middle eight and wonderful vocals from Richard more than compensate for a disappointingly pedestrian chorus. Here Richard was beginning to find not only his own voice, but also some worthy, contemporary outside material. Tim May's acoustic guitar is outstanding.

THAT'S WHAT I BELIEVE
(Carpenter/Phillips Oland)

An intro derived equally from the Hall & Oates hit, 'Maneater' and Stevie Wonder's 'Part Time Lover' and an astonishingly mature lead vocal from 15-year-old Scott Grimes make for an interesting track, and a minor album highlight.

Richard produced a complete album for Scott Grimes, which was released in the US and has been described as "a terrific début album for a youngster", but remains unreleased in the UK.

I'M STILL NOT OVER YOU
(Carpenter/Bettis)

Here's a strange thing: a Carpenter/Bettis composition that sounds more like Chicago than Chicago did... and in this case, that's no bad thing, for had this forceful ballad been released as a single, chart action would have surely resulted. As contemporary in its own way as the opening cut. Lead vocal: Richard Carpenter.

RICHARD CARPENTER
PIANIST · ARRANGER · COMPOSER · CONDUCTOR

Richard Carpenter: Pianist Arranger, Composer Conductor

RELEASED IN MARCH 1997 IN JAPAN AS POCM 1205

Prelude (Carpenter) / Yesterday Once More (Carpenter / Bettis)/Medley: Sing (Raposo) / Goodbye To Love (Carpenter / Bettis) / Eve (Carpenter / Bettis) / Rainy Days And Mondays (Williams / Nichols) / Look To Your Dreams (Carpenter / Bettis) / Superstar (Russell / Bramlett) / Someday (Carpenter / Bettis) / I Need To Be In Love (Carpenter / Bettis / Hammond) / Sandy (Carpenter / Bettis) / Time (Carpenter) For All We Know (Karlin / Wilson / James) / One Love (Carpenter / Bettis) Bless The Beasts And Children (De Vorzon / Botkin Jr.) / Flat Baroque (Carpenter) / All Those Years Ago (Carpenter / Phillips Oland) / Top Of The World (Carpenter / Bettis) / We've Only Just Begun (Williams / Nichols) / Karen's Theme (Carpenter)

Not so much easy listening as exceedingly superior elevator music, the fourteen tracks on this almost entirely instrumental CD comprise three new compositions plus eleven items (one a seven-tune medley) from the back catalogue of The Carpenters (including two titles from *Time*) performed exactly as the album title suggests, with Richard mostly supplying the 'vocals' on the piano. However, this doesn't appear to be a completely 'new' album, for

'Time' (from the solo album of the same name) seems to be the 1987 version, while two Carpenters songs, 'Sandy' and 'Flat Baroque', credit Karen with vocals and drums respectively, which - combined with a different engineering credit for these two titles - forces one to the conclusion that at least a part of the original recording has been used (in the case of 'Flat Baroque', almost certainly a large part of the original). Whilst there's a strong case for not messing with original recordings, if anyone has the right so to do, it must be the composer; and Richard's reworkings here are so radical as to be essentially alternate versions and, taken on their own undemanding terms, are in no way objectionable, though not exactly compelling. 'Prelude' and 'Karen's Theme', bookend the album in the manner of the old days, and are pleasant mood pieces, the latter more fully developed than the former, which in turn is rather more atmospheric. The only genuinely new song

(to most Carpenters aficionados) is 'All Those Years Ago', which was apparently recorded in the mid-Eighties by a Canadian artist named Veronique Beliveaux, for whom Richard Carpenter also produced an album, presumably during the same period.

Karen Carpenter
Karen Carpenter

A&M 31454-0588-2; RECORDED IN 1979, RELEASED IN 1996

During 1979, Richard Carpenter was neither in good enough health nor in the right frame of mind to make a new Carpenters album, but his sister was itching to get into the studio, and eventually decided to make a solo album without the umbilical cord/security blanket of his guiding hand. According to Richard's sleeve notes on the album when it was eventually released many years later, it was Herb Alpert who suggested Phil Ramone as producer for the project. Ramone had a varied, but interesting, list of production credits to his name: (alphabetically) Chicago, Billy Joel, Quincy Jones, Kenny Loggins, Groucho Marx (!), Paul Simon, Phoebe Snow, Barbra Streisand & Kris Kristofferson (on the soundtrack for A Star Is Born, etc). Obviously perfectly capable of doing the job well, perhaps his one handicap was that most of those in the above list were singer/songwriters who could provide their own material, which Karen was emphatically unable to do. Clearly, Ramone asked around, but the fact that several of the songs were written by musicians who played on the album suggests that he perhaps failed to spread his net wide enough...

Ultimately, this album has the dubious privilege of being the most disappointing and anti-climactic album of the entire career of The Carpenters. When it was not released at the time it was recorded, many felt (and some forcefully maintained) that Richard Carpenter had suppressed it, but he has always said that the album was not released in 1979/80 because it simply wasn't good enough, and in addition (and perhaps more significantly) that Karen was not unhappy about this.

Richard Carpenter: "They did a lot of recording, but it came down to A&M wanting them to do more recording. They wanted them to find some more material and by this time Karen had flown to New York enough, and Phil had flown to LA enough and they'd spent enough effort and money and she decided to shelve it. So I picked four tracks that I knew that she liked a great deal", which were remixed and included on *Lovelines*.

In Richard Carpenter's own words, the answer to why Karen made a solo album: "I think two reasons. One, I was taking some time off: I'd through the years gotten hung up on prescription sleeping pills and I had to go check myself in and get off them. This was in January of '79. I felt that she should be seeking some help herself and we could both get ourselves well and start the Eighties with a bang, but she wasn't ready to seek any help as far as the anorexia was concerned at the time.

She did not believe that she had it. So she had a lot of nervous energy, and wanted something to do because it was gonna take me a while to go through the programme and then to just convalesce. So I took 1979 off, and Karen decided on the solo album. I think that's one reason, the other is I really feel she wanted a little attention on her own. She wanted to be known, I guess, as other than part of the duo, not just as Karen of The Carpenters. I really think that meant something to her. As much as she loved working with me and the records and all of that... I'm sure there was some of that involved, so this would give her a chance to actually have a record that said 'Karen Carpenter'."

Jerry Moss: "I think she made her solo album basically because she wanted to work, and Richard for his own reasons wasn't able to work at the time, and she wanted to try something new. I think Phil Ramone will tell you that he tried to make an un-Carpenters record, and if that's your intent, then it really won't sound like a Carpenters record."

LOVELINES
(Temperton)

When Karen informed her brother that she was considering recording a solo album, he was understandably less than thrilled, but bestowed his approval, with one proviso: "don't do anything disco". His reaction on hearing this heavily disco-flavoured opening track wasn't recorded... but we can guess, and quite honestly, it's easy to understand the reasoning behind his embargo. After years of performing in The Carpenters' style, any step outside "the formula" would be traumatic, but given sympathetic material, something interesting would surely result. 'Lovelines' is, sadly, disco by numbers and even Karen's voice can't rescue an uninspired song and arrangement. A remixed version was the opener and title track of the 1989 album by The Carpenters. Rod Temperton is credited with "Rhythm and Vocal Arrangement" on the 'Lovelines' album version, and with "vocal acrobatics" on the 'Karen Carpenter' album.

ALL BECAUSE OF YOU
(Javors)

The acoustic arrangement here by Bob James is ambitious, probably too ambitious, forcing Karen into almost ungainly vocal phrasing over an instrumental track that is somewhat uninspired. Russell Javors was also credited as one of the guitarists on this album.

IF I HAD YOU
(Dorff/Harju/Herbstritt)

In Richard's opinion, this energetic track was the only possible hit single on the album, and the verses are pretty good, but these positive aspects are balanced by an over enthusiastic and strident chorus replete with an incisive horn pattern and a frightfully busy counter vocal arrangement. The sax breaks (by Michael Brecker) are also far too well-mannered, and Billy Joel fans will recognise the name of drummer Liberty DeVitto (sic). A remixed version of this song was included on *Lovelines*.

MAKING LOVE IN THE AFTERNOON
(Cetera)

That this is an album highlight may owe more to composer Peter Cetera's arrangement and vocal presence than Phil Ramone's production, and the fact that it somehow manages not to sound like a Chicago out-take. There's a real sense of energy and enjoyment here - from the Byrds-style guitar intro to the chorus vocals on the fade - that is sadly absent from the opening three cuts. This was a pairing that should have been investigated further.

IF WE TRY
(Temperton)

Pleasant without ever being at all inspiring, even the mid-song instrumental break of rousing horns can't breathe life into this mid-tempo stroll. As ever, Karen's lead is exemplary, but the material is somehow lacking. Again, a remixed version was included on *Lovelines*.

REMEMBER WHEN LOVIN' TOOK ALL NIGHT
(Farrar/Leiken)

One of Richard's main concerns regarding Karen's solo project was the choice of material, particularly self-consciously 'adult' songs such as this. Yes, it's pleasant enough, but somehow Karen singing explicitly about things which previously she'd merely implied doesn't sit well on the ear, nor do the breathy groans in the overlong fade - very subtle! The first-named songwriter is Australian John Farrar, an associate of Cliff Richard, The Shadows and Olivia Newton-John. A remixed version of this song was included on *Lovelines*.

STILL IN LOVE WITH YOU
(Javors)

Whilst musically this is much more forceful and interesting than the previous Javors offering, the lyric once again comes up short. With a rewrite, this could have been a strong contender for a hit single, having a strong contemporary edge that would have ensured radio airplay.

MY BODY KEEPS CHANGING MY MIND
(Pearl)

Alas, it's disco time again, and absolutely everybody involved - Karen included - sound like they're trying way too hard on this slight number. A remixed version appeared on *From The Top*, and Richard's sleeve notes are splendidly terse, the subtext being "I told you so".

MAKE BELIEVE IT'S YOUR FIRST TIME
(Morris/Wilson)

Immeasurably enhanced by a restrained arrangement and production, Karen's touchingly tentative appeal to a new love is the album's undoubted highlight. Without the cushion of backing vocals or harmonies, her unaccompanied voice conveys a wonderful sense of uncertainty and longing combined in this sensitive ballad, a far superior example of

the 'adult' material striven for (unsuccessfully) elsewhere on this album. This song is a great favourite among Carpenters fans, and was released as a single in Japan, although it is not known whether the version used was this one or the re-recorded version from *Voice Of The Heart*.

GUESS I JUST LOST MY HEAD
(Mounsey)

A largely undistinguished composition, production and performance, and all the more so in comparison with the preceding triumph. Perhaps anonymous would be a better word, for even with Karen's professional vocals, there's still no real spark of excitement or inspiration to be found here. Rob Mounsey is credited with keyboards, arrangement and orchestration.

STILL CRAZY AFTER ALL THESE YEARS
(Simon)

Paul Simon's navel-gazing classic is

given a radical overhaul and it's to the credit of the material that it manages to emerge with some credibility intact. Karen's vocal reading is suitably sympathetic, but once again Rob Mounsey's arrangement and orchestration (especially the backing vocals) are severely at odds with the material. As with 'Superstar', Karen felt uneasy with the original lyric, thus at her request Simon amended "crapped out" to "crashed out" in the middle eight. A remixed version was included on *From The Top*.

LAST ONE SINGIN' THE BLUES
(McCann)

A track not originally intended for inclusion on the album (and rightly so) is included here in unmixed form as a CD bonus. Taken at a lazy slope, Karen's vocal - excellent though it is - shows signs of being a guide, while her instructions to the band reveal her influence on the creative process. A curio, no more, although most fans reportedly regard this as special, perhaps because it was previously completely unheard, unlike many of the other tracks here.

The Singles   **1969-1973**

Compilations

The three most commercially successful compilation albums by The Carpenters are:

1. THE SINGLES 1969-1973
(A&M SP-3601; RELEASED 1973)

A 12 track album which topped the *Billboard* chart for a single week in 1974, was certified quadruple platinum by 1992, (and today is probably even more multi-platinum), and topped the UK album chart for 17 weeks between February and July, 1974.

2. THE SINGLES 1974-1978
(A&M AMLT-19748; RELEASED 1978)

Also a 12 track album, which was released in the UK, where it all but topped the chart in 1978/79, but was not released in the US. Both *Singles* albums include piano links between tracks, and a different version (not the single) of 'Can't Smile Without You' has been used on *1974 - 1978*.

3. ONLY YESTERDAY
(A&M SP-6601; RELEASED 1985)

A 20 track 'Greatest Hits' album including six remixed tracks ('Yesterday Once More', 'Superstar', 'Rainy Days And Mondays', 'Goodbye To Love', 'We've Only Just Begun' and 'Calling Occupants Of Interplanetary Craft') plus the single mix of 'Top Of The World'. This album topped the UK chart for seven weeks in 1990.

INTERPRETATIONS
A&M 31454 - 0312-2; RELEASED IN 1995

Released in 1994 as part of The Carpenters' 25th anniversary celebrations, this compilation differs from most in that none of the tracks included are Carpenter/Bettis or indeed Carpenter /anybody compositions, but rather interpretations of other songwriters' material, hence the title. To spice the mixture, three previously unreleased tracks were included.

Full track listing (previously unreleased songs noted *): Without A Song* / Sing / Bless The Beasts And Children / This Masquerade / Solitaire / When I Fall In Love / From This Moment On* / Tryin' To Get The Feeling Again* / When It's Gone / Where Do I Go From Here?/ Desperado / Superstar / Rainy Days And Mondays / Ticket To Ride / If I Had You / Please Mr. Postman / We've Only Just Begun / Calling Occupants of Interplanetary Craft / Little Girl Blue / You're The One / (They Long To Be) Close To You

WITHOUT A SONG
(Youmans/Rose/Eliscu)

The brevity (60 seconds) of this charming a cappella performance of a Twenties' standard is due to its being the opening section of a full version taken from The Carpenters' 1980 ABC TV Special, *Music, Music, Music*, that featured various guests.

FROM THIS MOMENT ON
(Porter)

Recorded for, but not used in, the same TV special as the previous entry, this duet for piano and voice is the studio version of a title featured on the *1976 Live At The Palladium* album, from which it differs hardly at all.

TRYIN' TO GET THE FEELING AGAIN
(Pomerantz)

This outtake from the *Horizon* sessions (not released due to a perceived adequate amount of ballads on that album) was misplaced for many years, until Richard found it in 1991, unmarked on the same tape reel as 'Only Yesterday'. Strings were added some three years later for inclusion on *Interpretations*. As with 'Now', Karen's lead is a guide vocal and has been deservedly described as "absolutely brilliant", and became a firm favourite among fans when it was released, perhaps a good reason for it being released as a single to mark the

25th anniversary of The Carpenters, when it briefly became a minor UK hit single. That Barry Manilow took the song into the US Top Ten little more than a year later is testament to Richard's ear for a good song.

THE COMPACT DISC COLLECTION

(A&M CAR CD 20; RELEASED 1989)

In late 1989, A&M Records released *The Compact Disc Collection*, a tastefully packaged (if somewhat impractical) limited edition boxed set containing 12 CDs. Each of the eleven original studio albums from *Ticket To Ride* (aka *Offering*) to *Lovelines* was included as a single CD, while the two Christmas albums, *Christmas Portrait* and *An Old Fashioned Christmas* were combined on a single 21 track CD.

Richard had remixed several tracks from earlier albums for this project ('A Song For You', 'Goodbye To Love', 'Calling Occupants...' etc), although the differences between originals and remixes were barely noticable. Other than remixes, no previously unreleased tracks were included. The

dozen CDs came in a 12"x 12" (LP-sized) white box which contained three thick white cardboard pages, each holding four naked CDs. Although the sturdy outer box provided some protection for the discs, they were not suspended above the cardboard "pages", and there is a suspicion that this style of packaging is less than ideal, and was adopted for marketing reasons rather than to ensure that the CDs remained in perfect condition. That said, the author has yet to discern any damage to the CDs in his copy of the box.

TRACK LISTING OF CHRISTMAS PORTRAIT

(+ denotes songs taken from *A Christmas Portrait*, *indicates songs taken from *An Old-Fashioned Christmas*)

It Came Upon A Midnight Clear* / Overture: 'Happy Holiday' etc* / An Old-Fashioned Christmas* / Christmas Waltz+ / Sleigh Ride+ / It's Christmas Time+ / Have Yourself A Merry Little Christmas+ / Santa Claus Is Comin' To Town+ / Christmas Song (Chestnuts Roasting...)+ / Carol Of The Bells+ /

Merry Christmas Darling+ / Christ Is Born+ / O Holy Night* / There's No Place Like Home For The Holidays* / Medley: 'Here Comes Santa Claus' etc* / Winter Wonderland, Silver Bells, White Christmas+ / Ave Maria+ / Selections From The Nutcracker (Omitting 'Trepak')* / Little Alter Boy* / I'll Be Home For Christmas+ / Silent Night+

BEST OF BEST + ORIGINAL MASTER KARAOKE
(RELEASED FEBRUARY 1992)

The interest in this Japanese compilation lies not in the regular version of the fifteen classics listed below, but rather in the same fifteen tracks presented on the second disc of the set in karaoke form: Richard personally remixed them all, removing the lead vocal of each (but retaining the backing vocals), resulting in a fascinating glimpse at the bare(ish) bones of the instrumental tracks... and of course providing a splendid opportunity for a good old-fashioned singalong. (The only other known example of an artist or band doing anything similar is the ultra-rare 1968 *Stack O'Tracks* album by The Beach Boys, which coincidentally also featured fifteen of their classics... only, being The Beach Boys, they also wiped the backing vocals as well!).

Track listing: Yesterday Once More / Superstar / Rainy Days And Mondays / Top Of The World / This Masquerade / I Won't Last A Day Without You / For All We Know / Jambalaya / Close To You / Hurting Each Other / Please Mr. Postman / Bless The Beasts And The Children / Goodbye To Love / I Need To Be In Love / We've Only Just Begun

MAGICAL MEMORIES OF THE CARPENTERS
(RELEASED 1993)

This 70 track 5CD set is still available via mail order from the Reader's Digest organisation and is, for those not too bothered with either owning every song or rarities, pretty much everything you could ask for (including the full live Bacharach/David medley previously only available on the 1989 Japanese *Anthology* 4CD set). The only slight disappointment is that the

songs are sequenced pretty much at random rather than presented chronologically. Every studio album is represented. This set is highly recommended by the official UK Carpenters fanzine, *Offering,* thus: "Recording quality and clarity excellent, much better than the 12 CD set"

IF I WERE A CARPENTER
(RELEASED AUGUST 1994)

Released on the 25th anniversary of The Carpenters' signing to A&M Records, and riding on the wave of The Carpenters' new found respect, this tribute album by a host of new, young and largely alternative musicians turned out to be a very patchy affair indeed: Matthew Sweet (with a small assist from Richard), Dishwalla and Grant Lee Buffalo turned in excellent re-interpretations, but sadly the rest of the performances were at best pedestrian, on the whole lamentable. If nothing else, at least they made you realise just how very fine the originals were.

Goodbye To Love (American Music Club) / Top Of The World (Shonen Knife) Superstar (Sonic Youth) / Close To You (Cranberries) / For All We Know (Bettie Serveert) / It's Going To Take Some Time This Time (Dishwalla) / Solitaire (Sheryl Crow) / Hurting Each Other (Johntte Napolitano with Marc Moreland) / Yesterday Once More (Redd Kross) / Calling Occupants Of Interplanetary Craft (Babes In Toyland) / Rainy Days And Mondays (Cracker) / Let Me Be The One (Matthew Sweet) / Bless The Beasts And The Children (4 Non Blondes) / We've Only Just Begun (Grant Lee Buffalo)

In addition, there are at least three compilations released only in Japan:

LIVE IN JAPAN:

A 2 CD set with a date of 1974 (presumably when it was recorded - release date uncertain)

TREASURES:

A 2 CD set of album tracks (as opposed to singles) released in 1987.

ANTHOLOGY:

A 4 CD set released in 1989.

Index